Tom Wolfe

Truman Capote

Norman Mailer

CHRIS ANDERSON

Style
as
Argument

Contemporary American Nonfiction

SOUTHERN ILLINOIS UNIVERSITY PRESS
Carbondale and Edwardsville

90 89 88 87   4 3 2 1

Library of Congress Cataloging-in-Publication Data

Anderson, Chris, 1955–
  Style as argument.

  Bibliography: p.
  Includes index.
  1. American prose literature–20th century–History
and criticism. 2. Reportage literature, American–
History and criticism. 3. Journalism–United States.
4. English language–Style. 5. Nonfiction novel–
History and criticism. 6. Narration (Rhetoric)
7. United States in literature. I. Title.
PS366.R44A5 1987   818'.508'09   86-21970
ISBN 0-8093-1314-6
ISBN 0-8093-1373-1 (pbk.)

For Barb, John, and Maggie

Contents

Acknowledgments

I want to thank a number of people for helping me write this book. As my teacher and dissertation director at the University of Washington, William Irmscher introduced me to the rhetorical criticism of nonfiction and later gave me very useful advice about the writing of books. Walter Beale was an invaluable colleague and friend at the University of North Carolina, Greensboro; his insightful reading of the first draft of the book led me to reconceive the purpose and implications of what I was doing. Keith Cushman of UNC-G also read the first draft and made several shrewd suggestions.

I sharpened my original ideas about nonfiction while teaching an experimental course at UNC-G in contemporary prose style; part of my argument in the last section of the Capote chapter is based on papers Lynn Snyder and Lana Whited wrote for that class.

I was able to revise and complete the manuscript during a semester's research assignment granted by the Vice Chancellor for Academic Affairs at UNC-G.

Dennis Rygiel of Auburn University, John Clifford of the University of North Carolina, Wilmington, and Charles Schuster of the University of Wisconsin, Milwaukee read the manuscript for Southern Illinois University Press and made many useful suggestions. Kenney Withers of Southern Illinois University Press has been a prompt, fair, and reassuring editor. Dan Gunter of SIU Press did a fine job of copyediting the manuscript.

Finally, without the patience and sympathy of my wife, I would have never been able to write the book at all. She took care of the kids while I was writing, listened to my monologues, and weathered my ups and downs. Dedicating this book to her, and to the kids, is the least I can do.

Portions of chapter 2 appeared in a different form in *The Midwest Quarterly*, vol. 28, no. 3 (Spring 1987). An extension and application of chapter 4 appeared in *The Journal of Advanced Composition*, vol. 7, no. 1 (1986).

Style
as
Argument

Introduction: *The Tacit Statement*

Form always makes one tacit statement—it says: I am
a definite form of existence, I choose to have character
and quality, I choose to be recognizable, I am—
everything considered—the best that could be done
under the circumstances, and so superior to a blob.

—Norman Mailer, *Cannibals and Christians* (370)

The language of contemporary American nonfiction is not transparent but translucent. We are never able to look completely past
the words on the page to the people and events they evoke; we are
always aware of the words themselves, of their rhythms and their
textures. Our experience reading contemporary nonfiction is an
experience of style. In the four individual studies that make up this
book I try to recreate and interpret this experience through a close
reading of the major nonfiction of Tom Wolfe, Truman Capote,
Norman Mailer, and Joan Didion. The book is an effort to characterize the distinctive styles of these writers and to show how the
richness and complexity of their prose discloses an important argument about the value of language itself.

Although a few substantial books have been written about the
"New Journalism" and the "Nonfiction Novel," there has been
little of the kind of practical criticism of nonfiction texts that I

1

undertake here. Previous studies have been concerned with the larger question of genre, with the relationship between fiction and nonfiction, literature and journalism. These are important issues, and in the course of my own analysis I will have something to say about them. It will be clear in my readings that I side with John Hollowell, Ronald Weber, and John Hellman in disputing Mas'ud Zavarzadeh's claims about the nature of nonfiction as a "zero-degree" interpretative form. Yet I will agree with Zavarzadeh that nonfiction prose is one of the principal rhetorical genres of the age and that it is inextricably connected with the effort to express the force and magnitude and sheer overpowering energy of the American experience.

I will also try to develop another, more important claim about genre in the course of the interpretations that follow. In my view nonfiction reportage is more than informative: it is an effort to persuade us to attitudes, interpretations, opinions, even actions. The rhetoric of reportage is subtle—it must be interpreted, the texts read carefully for nuances of imagery and tone—but it is there, powerful and persuasive. Hollowell, Weber, and Hellman have demonstrated that the use of point of view, symbolism, and other literary techniques makes the New Journalism inherently and consciously "fictive." Only a naïve reader, they suggest, ever regarded *The Electric Kool-Aid Acid Test* or *In Cold Blood* as literally true or free of the author's shaping attitudes and perceptions. The argument I will make is that these broadly "literary" devices are perhaps more importantly rhetorical strategies for shaping the reader's attitudes and perceptions. At least since Wayne Booth's *Rhetoric of Fiction*, we have known that everything an author "shows" will serve to "tell," which is to say that the dramatic presentations of contemporary prose tacitly argue for values and attempt to persuade us to adopt those values.

More than that, it seems to me that nonfiction reportage has taken over many of the rhetorical responsibilites of other genres in recent American culture. Seymour Krim goes so far as to say that nonfiction is the "defacto literature of our time" (183). Wolfe proclaims, with characteristic hyperbole, that in the fifties and sixties the New Journalism "seized the power" from the novel and continued the traditions of social realism in the forms of reportage ("New Journalism" 23). Summarizing the critical consensus of the last three decades, Weber explains that in addition to "fabulation" or "irrealism," "metafiction," and science fiction, the nonfiction novel is generally regarded as one of the primary alternatives in contemporary discourse to the narrative conventions of the traditional novel (9–12). In broader historical terms it can be argued that recent nonfiction participates in what Richard Weaver calls the movement from "inference" to "reportage" in the history of rhetoric ("The Spaciousness of the Old Rhetoric"), or what Booth describes as the shift from telling to showing in the development of modern narrative technique (*Rhetoric of Fiction*). Contemporary nonfiction values concrete detail. It avoids the "generic," refusing to "infer" values, as Weaver would put it, and thus to engage in open deliberation on moral issues. Its growing prestige reflects the epistemological skepticism of the contemporary mind, the modern demand for the narration of fact rather than explicit generalization and commentary, even though in the nuanced language of writers like Wolfe, Capote, Mailer, and Didion rhetoric has not been eliminated but rather reconstituted in subtler and more concrete forms. From this perspective the critical issue extends beyond the intrinsic literary merit of nonfiction prose; the more important question is the role of nonfiction as a form in the cultural and ethical debate of our time.

But my intention in this book is not to establish an epistemological framework for understanding the genre of nonfiction or to consider in a purely theoretical way the place of nonfiction in the history of discourse. Because I believe that contemporary prose is rich and interesting in itself—because I believe that its significance lies in the translucence of its language—my discussions feature the important texts of the genre, concentrate on subtleties and details of style. My method is what Bernard Brock and Robert Scott in their *Methods of Rhetorical Criticism* call "eclectic and experiential": rather than trying to develop a unified rhetorical theory, I borrow freely from both classical and contemporary rhetorical and literary theory whenever it suits the immediate purposes of my argument. Although I draw on Aristotle and

Wolfgang Iser, Cicero and Chaim Perelman, Longinus and Kenneth Burke, as well as on the critical theorizing of Wolfe, Capote, Mailer, and Didion themselves, I have subordinated theory to a consideration of style and theme in individual works. My project is to engage contemporary nonfiction in its own terms, registering first and second impressions, noting recurring strategies and images, assembling striking details and anomalies. I want in this book to take the next step in the study of nonfiction discourse, not arguing in the abstract for the value of the genre but dramatizing that value through concrete, inductive readings of actual texts.

In each chapter I focus on a strategy or set of strategies unique to that individual author: Wolfe's rhetorical intensifications and strategies of presence, Capote's authorial silences, Mailer's self-dramatizations and metadiscourse, Didion's radical particularity. But while the chapters can be read independently as separate stylistic studies, they also build on each other. I establish the controlling tensions in the chapter on Wolfe, try in the next chapter to link these tensions with Capote's strategy of authorial detachment, then show how the subtle paradoxes of style in Wolfe and Capote become an explicit polemic in Mailer, and finally, test and qualify my analysis in the work of Didion. Each chapter varies in structure and comprehensiveness, depending on the demands of my argument at that point and the nature of that author's work. I do not consider Mailer's novels, for example, because they are not relevant to the point I want to make, although I do consider Capote's fiction as a way of emphasizing my argument about the function of implicitness in nonfiction. A number of other authors could easily fit into my study: John Hersey, James Agee, Michael Herr, E. B. White, Lewis Thomas, Richard Selzer, Annie Dillard. I have chosen to focus on Wolfe, Capote, Mailer, and Didion simply because they seem to me the most significant and representative figures among the increasingly large group of important contemporary journalists and essayists and because their work seems to lend itself best to extended and detailed treatment.

My central concern in interpreting this work is the relationship between style and theme. Form is the shape of content, Ben Shahn has said. In contemporary nonfiction, as in all literature, style is best understood as a reflection and enactment of a content and a point of view. In fact, I will try to show that the principal theme of contemporary nonfiction is its own rhetorical dilemma. The writing of Wolfe, Capote, Mailer, and Didion is profoundly metadiscursive, concerned with the problems of style and expression and language in America, and in this way it provides all the terms we need for understanding its internal workings and its cultural value. What preoccupies all four writers, whatever their ostensible subject, is the effort to convey in words the inexplicable energies, intensities, and contradictions of American experience. Though in very different ways, Wolfe, Capote, Mailer, and Didion each define their subjects as somehow beyond words—antiverbal or nonverbal, threatening or sublime, overpowering and intense or private and intuitive—and then repeatedly call our attention to the issue of inexplicability throughout their descriptions and expositions. A self-consciousness about the limits of language is the structuring principle of their work. Wordlessness can be positive or negative in these texts, energizing or threatening. It can be personal or communal. It is something to fight and something to claim. Yet whatever its nature, it generates a rhetorical challenge for the writer. As they themselves define their task, Wolfe, Capote, Mailer, and Didion must push language to its limits, explore the edges of expression, intensify and expand the power of words to reach the level of a sublime and inexplicable object.

The story I will tell in this book is the story of how the dialectic between words and wordlessness develops over the course of specific texts, how it determines the distinctive styles of each author, how it conditions our responses as readers—and how, ultimately, it is subsumed in a larger irony. Because the experiences which the New Journalists must describe are wordless, beyond language, their language must ultimately "fail." Yet I will argue that the language of Wolfe, Capote, Mailer, and Didion is stylistically successful: complex, nuanced, layered, affecting, always aware of itself as style, as form, as artifice. My underlying purpose is to explore the rhetorical consequences of this stylishness, this awareness of style, this translucence. As my analysis unfolds I want not only to explain the central strategies and forms of contemporary American nonfiction but also to demonstrate how its rhetorical self-consciousness prepares us to regard style itself as argument, a tacit but powerful statement about the value of form as form, style as style.

In the end I hope that my rhetorical approach to these issues will contribute to our understanding of Wolfe, Capote, Mailer, and Didion as important literary figures. On this level I have in mind an audience of literary critics and Americanists, as well as a small but growing number of specialists in the New Journalism and the nonfiction novel. At the same time I hope that the book will be of interest to teachers of writing and to theorists in rhetoric and composition. I first became interested in contemporary nonfiction as a writing teacher struggling to make my students understand the notion of voice and style as values in themselves; I started working on this project because I was convinced that, as Dennis Rygiel has recently argued, rhetoric and composition needs a thorough critique of the kind of nonfiction prose that fills freshman readers—the discourse that in effect defines current rhetorical theory as a field of interest. In its preoccupation with the processes of composing, useful as this has been for reviving interest in writing, current rhetorical theory has not given enough serious attention to the products of these processes.

My reading of Wolfe, Capote, Mailer, and Didion has no immediate classroom applications, although I develop terms that might be helpful in explaining the basic strategies of contemporary style to our students. The usefulness of this study for rhetoric and composition, I think, is *as* literary and rhetorical criticism. It is easy to lose sight of the larger meaning of what we do as we work to teach writing day by day. Nonfiction prose becomes simply a source of quick and disposable examples for illustrating this or that stylistic device. I will make no further comments in the rest of this book about the teaching of writing, but everything I say can finally be read as an effort to show that the value of nonfiction extends beyond the truncating categories of the freshman reader. Like the poetry and fiction we teach in our other classes, contemporary prose has a value in itself. Perhaps an appreciation of nonfiction as a literary and rhetorical genre will help deepen and sustain our enthusiasm for the teaching of writing. Perhaps, too, it will help keep the discipline of rhetoric and composition from becoming nothing more than a pseudoscience on the one hand or a mere exercise-exchange on the other.

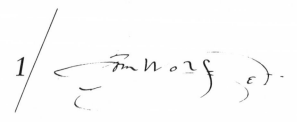

Pushing the Outside of the Envelope

I

In his essay on the New Journalism Wolfe seems quite confident in the power of language to make experience present on the page. Using the devices of the realistic novel, he claims, a writer can not only render the full details of a scene or event but also describe "the subjective, emotional life of the characters" (21). Freed from the stodgy conventions of traditional journalism, Wolfe seems to be saying, language can penetrate to the heart of things. The rhetorical virtuosity of his own prose seems to embody this confidence. His genius for scene-by-scene reconstruction, his ear for dialogue and mimicry, his ability to manipulate sentence structure apparently at will, all give the impression that Wolfe is completely at home in language, able to do exactly what he wants to do when he wants to do it. He seems to delight in wringing out the rhetorical possibilities of words.

The test pilots in *The Right Stuff* use an interesting metaphor to describe what they do: "pushing the outside of the envelope." The "envelope" is a flight test term for "the limits of a particular aircraft's performance, how tight a turn it could make at such-and-such a speed, and so on." To "push the outside of the envelope" is to "probe the outer limits" of an aircraft's speed and maneuverability, to discover its capabilities and power, to see how far and fast it can go (12). Wolfe's project is to push the outside of the envelope of language. Like the fighter jocks he celebrates, he probes the limits of his machinery with a kind of cocky enthusiasm, a great confidence in the quickness of his reflexes and the sureness of his instincts.

But underneath Wolfe's energy and abandon is an awareness that language is finally incapable of encompassing reality. The subject of his writing is always the language of the experience he is addressing as much as the experience itself. He is fascinated with the insider's slang, the power words of the privileged groups and underground cultures he seeks out. He loves to mimic private jargons, and he repeatedly comments on the cultural, political, and psychological dimensions of particular phrases and conjuring words. Despite his claims for the purely mimetic function of the New Journalism, his own writing is metadiscursive. While he is not "sailing off to Lonesome Island on a Tarot boat" ("New Journalism" 31), writing about writing as an escape from the intensity of experience, his work is in a very important sense *about* language and the possibilities of form. And what seems to concern him most is the inability of language to describe certain central experiences which he regards as private, intuitive, and on several levels both sublime and religious. He continually calls our attention to the ineffable, either explicitly, in narrative exposition, or implicitly, in the dramatized rhetorical situations of his characters.

In "Las Vegas (What?) Las Vegas (Can't hear you! Too noisy) Las Vegas!!!" the first essay in his first book, *The Kandy-Kolored Tangerine-Flake Streamline Baby*, Wolfe is concerned with the complex, bizarre and mind-numbing sublimity of Las Vegas and all it represents. I mean sublimity here in its classical sense. The kind of sensory overload Wolfe describes in this essay is sublime: intense, powerful, overwhelming; in the end, beyond words. The title itself suggests the way in which the sheer volume of the experience overwhelms language. The "wheeps" and "urps" of piped-in pop music combine with the incessant sound of slot machines and excited voices to create an atmosphere of "electronic jollification" in which "mere words are beaten back like old atonal Arturo Toscanini trying to sing along with the NBC Symphony" (14).

Electronic jollification is a good phrase for the visual stimulus of Las Vegas as well—the "inevitable buttocks decolletage" of the "ack-ack" girls in their "incarnadine stretch pants" (13–14), the soaring, swiveling, oscillating neon signs (8). Las Vegas has "succeeded in wiring an entire city with this electronic stimulation, day and night, out in the middle of the desert" (7).

It is arguable whether this kind of experience is lofty or grand or elevated enough to be sublime in Longinus' sense. Wolfe is rejecting conventional notions of sublimity and beauty and celebrating the low-rent and the tacky—perhaps we should call this the ironic sublime. Yet it is clear that he sees in the underside of American culture something powerful and vast. Despite his partly ironic tone, he is caught up in the "magnitude of the achievement" of Las Vegas, impressed by the way it "magnifies," "foliates," "embellishes" sensory stimulus (8). "In this town," he quotes from the president of the Dune's Casino, "you've got to move ahead in quantum jumps": "Quantum? But exactly! The beauty of the Dune's Casino de Paris show is that is will be beyond art, beyond dance, beyond spectacle, even beyond the titillations of the winking crotch. The Casino de Paris will be a behemoth piece of American calculus, like Project Mercury" (17). What compels Wolfe about Las Vegas is its size and scope. He is drawn to it because it exceeds the normal and everyday, exceeds even spectacle.

In "The Kandy-Kolored Tangerine-Flake Streamline Baby," the title essay on the custom car culture in California, Wolfe shifts terms slightly. He is still interested in the tremendous, the bizarre, the chaotic. In the opening scene he describes the "wild" and "electrified" atmosphere of a custom car show in Burbank, where two hundred "bouffant nymphs" "ricochet" across the platform dancing the "bird, the hully-gully and the shampoo" while a Chris-Craft cruiser goes round and round in an enormous pool in the center of the showroom (76–77). Here is another McLuhanesque scene of simultaneity and electronic intensity. But as the description proceeds Wolfe seems more and more fascinated by the specifically religious dimensions of the customizers. In their pursuit of a new "baroque" style of design for the automobile, the customizers become a true "cult," devoted like true artists to a private vision. And they strike Wolfe as mysterious and alien, inexplicable. They are "buried in the alien and suspect underworld of California youth." They're like "Easter Islanders," he says. "Suddenly you come upon the astonishing objects, and then you have to figure out how they got there and why they're there" (85).

This is the dynamic of Wolfe's reporting throughout *Streamline Baby*. He is the explorer suddenly coming upon astonishing objects, and his essays are attempts to figure out how these objects got there and why. The religious allusions and imagery here are important. Wolfe's strategy is to portray his subject as in some way removed and beyond. He creates a distance between the subject and his attempts to describe it. "We're out on old Easter Island," he says again of the customizers, "in the buried netherworld of teen-age Californians, and those objects, those cars, they have to do with the gods and the spirit and a lot of mystic stuff in the community" (86).

The rhetorical implications of this kind of allusion become clear in *The Electric Kool-Aid Acid Test*. Wolfe is again attracted by the intense and the bizarre. The drug culture of Kesey's pranksters is lavish and spectacular, its style psychedelic, jumbled, nonlinear. Wolfe is again caught up in spectacle—in a broad sense, the sublime. And because these experiences are sublime—at the edges of experience, unusual, bold and overwhelming—they strain and exceed language. In any sublime experience, by definition, language breaks down after a certain point. The failure of language is an index to the grandeur or magnitude of the event or object. Kesey's "considerable new message," his "current fantasy," must somehow be told, Wolfe says. Kesey is not just a prankster but a prophet intent on converting others to his vision. "But how to tell it" [the fantasy]? "It has never been possible, has it, truly, just to come out and *announce* the fantasy?" (35). Wolfe asks the same question several pages later after trying to describe Kesey's vision: "Beautiful! . . . the current fantasy . . . But how to tell them?—about such arcane little matters as Captain Marvel and The Flash . . . *The Life*—and the very *Superkids*—" (38).

"How to tell them?" "How to tell it?" becomes a refrain in *Acid Test*. Wolfe's concern is not only with the special quality of the prankster's experience but with the rhetorical problem of trying to communicate that experience. "How could you tell anyone about it?" (40), he repeatedly asks, speaking in part in the voice of the pranksters themselves: "And by and by, of course, the citizens of La Honda and others would start wondering . . . what are the ninnies *doing*? How to tell it? But there was no way to tell them about *the experience*. You couldn't put it into words" (65). Throughout *Acid Test* Wolfe focuses on Kesey's attempts to explain his vision to outsiders—the Unitarians, the Hell's Angels, reporters like Wolfe, the mundane and bourgeois populace.

In a crucial chapter, Wolfe explains the problem in explicitly religious terms. The center of the prankster's shared vision is the "Unspoken Thing," an inexplicable mental ecstasy. "They made a point of not putting it into words," because "to put it into so many words, to define it, was to limit it." Language would translate the nonlinear into the linear, the simultaneous into the sequential, the infinite into the finite. Thus Kesey's language is "cryptic," metaphorical, consisting of parables and aphorisms. He practices the rhetoric of silence, refusing to explain or teach explicitly (127).

But more than that, the Unspoken Thing *can't* be described. Like Christianity and Buddhism and all the major world religions, the religion of the pranksters is founded on an "overwhelming *new experience*," an experience of the "holy," of "possession by the deity" (128). Wolfe grants that the pranksters have no theology, no philosophy that can be reduced to an ism, that they don't in fact believe in a hereafter or in any kind of salvation. What makes them religious is that they have shared a flash of private and intuitive insight. They have all lived a moment of transcendence.

Because this moment of ecstasy is an *experience*, it defies explanation. Augustine realized the circularity of religious belief and in his *On Christian Doctrine*, actually an analysis of the rhetoric of religion, tried to propose rhetorical strategies for breaking that circle. The problem is that if we don't first have the experience of faith, we will not understand or attend to a speaker's attempt to analyze the experience or persuade us to accept God's presence in the world—*crede ut intelligas*, he repeatedly quotes from Isaiah: you must believe in order to understand. Quoting from Joachim Wach, Max Weber, and other sociologists and theologians, Wolfe in this chapter is making the same point. Kesey's actions as leader of the pranksters parallel the actions and style of any prophet or leader of a religious group; the pranksters themselves behave exactly like any cult or religious following, performing rituals and adopting special languages much like the early Christians. But the important point for Wolfe is that the pranksters, like all religious groups, are faced with the problem of trying to communicate experiences that are by definition incommunicable. "You're either on the bus or off the bus." You either know, or you don't. Only insiders, only those who have experienced the kairos, the moment, for themselves can understand what the pranksters are trying to achieve.

The Right Stuff is an investigation of language on many levels. Wolfe's interest is in the rhetoric of the space program: the rhetoric of politicians warning the country of Soviet domination in space, the rhetoric of the press idealizing the character and accomplishments of the Mercury astronauts, the rhetoric of the astronauts themselves as they fight to call their "capsule" a "spacecraft." But here too the underlying issue is the inexplicability of the experience Wolfe is trying to describe. The adventures of the fighter jocks and the astronauts are unparalleled. The job of the test pilot is to push the outside of the envelope, take his plane beyond the edge of known experience. What he perceives in the cockpit is privileged: no one else has ever had the opportunity to know what he knows. It is also intense, violent, spectacular, often overwhelming—planes tumbling end over end at the upper reaches of the atmosphere, the air thinning to blackness at the edge of space. "My God!" Wolfe explains, "it was impossible to explain to an outsider." The joys of the right stuff are "ineffable," true "mysteries" (151).

As in *Acid Test*, Wolfe devotes a central chapter of *The Right Stuff* to an explicit discussion of this rhetorical problem. The distinction, in part, is between the actual experience of the right stuff—of being a fighter pilot and experiencing, for example, night landings on an aircraft carrier—and any prior effort to describe that experience in language. "To say that an F-4 was coming back onto this heaving barbecue from out of the sky at a speed of 135 knots," Wolfe observes, "might have been the truth in the training lecture, but it did not begin to get across the idea of what the newcomer saw from the deck itself." During an actual landing, "one experienced a neural alarm that no lecture could have prepared him for" (27). Nor could the pilot himself begin to explain why he would give up the chance for a safe career in business and continue risking his life in high performance military aircraft. "He couldn't explain it . . . the very words for it had been amputated." The young pilot was "like the preacher in *Moby Dick* who climbs up into the pulpit on a rope ladder and then pulls the ladder up behind him; except the pilot could not use the words necessary to express the vital lesson" (34). The sensations of flight, then, are, difficult if not impossible to describe; and the quality of the fighter jock himself, his underlying motivations, his sense of himself, is also "ineffable" (24).

At stake in the right stuff is a quality of "*manliness, manhood, manly courage,*" something "ancient, primordial, irresistible" (29). The fighter jock was drawn to flying by a sense of its manly challenge. It tested him in a special way, giving him the opportunity to demonstrate courage and control in what Wolfe later calls "single warrior combat." Furthermore, having such courage was a matter of "election." Those with the right stuff were set apart as gifted and unique. "A man either had it or he didn't! There was no such thing as having most of it" (29). Flight school was designed not to train a pilot but to find out which candidates had the right stuff and which didn't: "All the hot young fighter jocks began trying to test the limits themselves in a superstitious way. They were like believing Presbyterians of a century before who used to probe their own experience to see if they were truly among *the elect*" (30). In *Acid Test* the religious parallel is with mysticism; here it is with Calvinism. But the suggestion is that both the pranksters and the fighter jocks are insiders with a privileged insight or special talent not accessible to others. The fighter jocks make up a "true fraternity" of pilots blessed with that "indefinable, unutterable, integral stuff" (30).

It's not just that the right stuff is inexplicable. It's that discussing the right stuff, even if it were possible, is unmanly. The unwritten code of the fighter pilots is that feelings—joy, courage, fear—

are not to be talked about. The pilot and the astronaut are models of the stereotypical American strong-silent male. "To talk about it [the right stuff] in so many words was forbidden, of course. The very words *death, danger, bravery, fear* were not to be uttered except in the occasional specific instance or for ironic effect" (34). Rather than be guilty of betraying unmanly exhilaration or fear, the pilots learned to describe their experiences indirectly through various "codes" and ironically understated stories: "They diced that righteous stuff up into little bits, bowed ironically to it, stumbled blindfolded around it, groped, lurched, belched, staggered, bawled, sang, roared, and feinted at it with self-deprecating humor. Nevertheless!—they never mentioned it by name" (35–36).

Wolfe later calls this form of expression "Pygmalion in reverse." While the press inflates and idealizes the story of the Mercury astronauts, indulging in sentimental hyperbole, the true pilot always underplays the danger he might be in, drawling in his Chuck Yeager, West Virginia accent about the "little ol' red light up here on the control panel" even when the plane is close to plunging into the ocean. Understatement demonstrates, through a kind of negative logic, the true bravery of the pilot. "We've obviously got a man up there in the cockpit who doesn't have a nerve in his body! He's a block of ice! He's made of 100 percent righteous victory-rolling True Brotherly stuff" (68).

All this obviously has consequences for Wolfe himself. In dramatizing the rhetorical situation of his characters, in repeatedly calling attention to religious parallels and their implications for language, Wolfe is alerting us to the tension underlying his own efforts as a reporter. First, Wolfe ultimately cannot describe the subjects he takes up, for all the reasons that his characters cannot describe their experience. If the experience is truly ineffable, it ultimately resists even Wolfe's attempts to describe it. Second, even if he did succeed in describing these subjects, that success would in itself label him as an outsider: since the experience of the pranksters and the astronauts is fundamentally nonverbal and even antiverbal, the journalist is by definition—by virtue of the fact that he is writing a book, in whatever form, at whatever level of sympathy and engagement—an outsider, someone who is not on the bus, someone who does not have the right stuff. For Kesey, writing is an "old-fashioned and artificial form" (104) "trap[ping] us in syntax" (154). The reporters who do come out to Kesey's commune to try to interpret the fantasy for the middle-classers in La Honda are humiliated and frustrated: "All right, Film Editor, Article Writer, Participant-Observer, you're here," Wolfe mockingly exhorts. "On with your . . . editing writing observing" (158). Clearly this exhortation has implications for Wolfe's own situation as a participant-observer. In *The Right Stuff* reporters are outside "all the unspoken things": "The real problem was that reporters violated the invisible walls of the fraternity. They blurted out questions and spoke boorish words about . . . all the unspoken things!—about fear and bravery (they would say the words!) and how you *felt* at such-and-such a moment! It was obscene! They presumed a knowledge and an intimacy they did not have and had no right to" (62). Wolfe is commenting here on his own enterprise. He too is speaking the unspoken words and violating the invisible walls. His effort is to achieve an intimacy with his subject that might enable him to recreate it for his readers, and this effort, he is saying, is intrinsically suspect.

In an author's note at the end of *Acid Test* Wolfe says that he has "tried not only to tell what the pranksters did but to re-create the mental atmosphere or subjective reality of it." What I'm suggesting is that throughout *Acid Test*, and throughout *Streamline Baby* and *The Right Stuff*, Wolfe persistently argues that this enterprise is impossible. He sets out to be an insider having established almost from the beginning that the particular kinds of experiences he is trying to enter into defy words.

II

Under the pressure of this rhetorical situation, Wolfe must push the outside of the envelope himself, take language to its limits. Wolfe does not turn away from the inexplicable or sidestep it. He takes it head on. To understand Wolfe we need to see him defining his subject as unattainable and then testing his powers against it. He is a daredevil, in a sense, always seeking out the impossible. And to suggest the intensity and magnitude, the complexity and grandeur of his subject, he must make his language more intense. He must magnify the conventional devices of language, juice them up, to reach the level of his subject.

As Wolfe explains in the introduction to *Streamline Baby*, it is partly a question of imitative form. The new "baroque style" of the subcultures he's discovered demands a new baroque form of prose. "The thing was," he says, "I knew I had another story all the time, a bona fide story, the real story of the Hot Rod & Custom Car show, but I didn't know what to do with it. It was outside the system of ideas I was used to working with" (xi). What he calls "the new style of life" requires a new style of writing; "free forms" of living require free forms of expression (xvi, xvii). He makes the same point in "The New Journalism." The "pale beige tone" of the conventional journalist is no longer appropriate for describing a psychedelic culture (17). Style must be a response to the material, and the material here is powerful, nonlinear, unconventional.

Of course, there is nothing really new about this. Longinus describes exactly the same dynamic in the treatise *On the Sublime*. The rhetoric of the sublime in his view is a natural response to the intensity, even the terror, of the sublime experience. In the face of the vast or chaotic or overwhelming the writer naturally becomes enthusiastic, excited, breathless; to draw the reader in, suggest the nature of the experience, the writer must magnify the figures of normal rhetorical presentation. In the rhetoric of the sublime, "imitation approaches the effects of nature" (103); the boundlessness, the vastness, the transcendence of the object lead to "enthusiasm" in writing, to a "passion" and even a "frenzy" which flashes forth from the sentences and "scatters everything before it like a thunderbolt" (59, 43).

In other words, there is a rhetorical logic to the kind of intensity and the abundance of figures we will be seeing in Wolfe's prose. All descriptive, informative writing aims at making the subject "present" to the reader, to use the term of the contemporary rhetorician Chaim Perelman. When the subject is within the realm of everyday expression, it can be made present without amplification or intensification. But when the subject exceeds language, when it is sublime and even ineffable, the writer can make it present, if at all, only by resorting to all the various strategies in the rhetorical repertoire for magnifying presence—repetition, alliteration, hypotyposis, amplification, enumeration, and so on.

Let's consider in some detail three passages from three stages in Wolfe's career, each clearly written under the pressure of the inexplicable or the sublime. Each is one of those central moments of direct evocation around which Wolfe builds his narratives.

The first is a description of casino signs and buttocks decolletage from "Las Vegas" (8–10). Wolfe has just suggested that what characterizes the Las Vegas experience is a "quixotic inflammation of the senses," a magnifying of sensual stimulation, both visual and sexual. He has defined his object as sublime. He then turns to giving several examples, and in the process draws on a battery of rhetorical strategies for enlivening his prose. The passage is virtually an illustration of many of the techniques that both Longinus and Perelman catalogue for creating greater presence in language:

Repetition.   Las Vegas, Wolfe says, is not made up of buildings or of trees, but "signs." From a mile away on Route 91 all you can see are "signs"—no buildings, no trees. "Such signs!" In repeating "sign" three times, Wolfe attempts to make the image increasingly present in the mind of the reader. Repetition, as Perelman suggests, is the most basic and in some ways the most effective device of presence (174). It is not enough in Wolfe to say something once; that doesn't begin to suggest the real impression of the experience he is trying to describe. To fix it in the reader's mind, to keep it in the foreground of the reader's consciousness, he must find ways of repeating certain details in various forms, securing the field of attention for that one impression.

In the next two paragraphs he seizes on the image of the "buttocks decolletage" to describe the odd sexual styles of this subculture and then repeats the phrase at least half a dozen times—"the Las Vegas buttocks decolletage," "to achieve buttocks decolletage," "all around me the decolletage-bare backside," "pregnant brunette . . . with buttocks decolletage aft," "the chic of wearing buttocks decolletage" and so on. Simply featuring one element from a scene endows that element with a certain presence. Repetition magnifies that presence, "overestimating" the declaration, making it louder or more noticeable, so to speak. What is repeated often enough and strongly enough cannot be ignored.

Amplification. The casino signs do not simply "tower." They "tower. They revolve, they oscillate, they soar in shapes before which the existing vocabularly of art history is helpless." Wolfe is not content to supply one verb, one predicate, one clause. Instead he expands the action into three subsequent independent clauses, emphasizing the movement of the signs through structural repetition. He is not content to supply one example of the signs that dominate the skyline. Instead he provides a long accumulating list: "Boomerang Modern, Palette Curvilinear, Flash Gordon Ming-Alert Spiral, McDonald's Hamburger Parabola, Mint Casino Elliptical, Miami Beach Kidney."

The idea is not logically advanced by such accumulations; as readers we understand the basic notion after the general statement itself. The list creates presence by amplifying the original thesis. As Longinus explains, "amplification . . . is an aggregation of all the constituent parts and topics of a subject, lending strength to the argument by dwelling upon it" (77). Wolfe's underlying meaning is constant throughout these long sentences and series. The variations he effects do not change it in kind. Neither do they explain or justify it. The particulars in the series are really alternate versions of the same assertion, concretizations of the subject which imply the same predicate. But just by this implicit rephrasing of the original proposition, Wolfe succeeds in conveying the impression of amplitude. He dwells on the subject and thus causes us to dwell on it. He suggests its depth and breadth. We have the impression he is casting around for more and more appropriate examples and illustrations, drawing almost random particulars from the wealth of detail in the scene to somehow convey its reality.

The union of figures for a common object. Closely related to both repetition and amplification is the piling up of several figures to describe the same idea or image. Las Vegas high school "buds," he observes, have copied the show-girl fashion of flesh-tight slacks:

> They achieve the effect of having been dipped once, briefly, in Helenca stretch nylon. More and more they look like those wonderful old girls out of Flash Gordon who were wrapped just once over in Baghdad pantaloons of clear polyethylene with only Flash Gordon between them and the insane red-eyed assaults of the minions of Ming. It is as if all the hip young suburban gals of America named Lana, Deborah and Sandra, who gather wherever the arc lights shine and the studs steady their coiffures in the plate-glass reflection, have convened in Las Vegas with their bouffant hair above and anatomically stretch-pant-swathed little bottoms below, here on the new American frontier. But exactly! (10)

Each of the three sentences in this paragraph offers a different simile or comparison for describing the same phenomenon. Wolfe can't convey the impression he is after through one image; he must multiply figures, add, intensify—all these devices Longinus calls varieties of "intensification" (75). And each simile is more detailed and elaborate, the power of one carrying over into the next.

Accumulating sentence structures.   Notice in the paragraph above how the sentences also become longer and more elaborate. Wolfe lengthens the modifying elements surrounding the base sentence as he proceeds, moving from "briefly," in the first, to the long "who were wrapped just once" clause in the second, to the still longer "named Lana, Deborah . . . who gather wherever" in the third. Sentence structure reflects amplifications and climaxes. Stripped of their modifiers these sentences simply convey information. The series and extensions of detail that take place in the added phrases and clauses lengthen the sentence and the time it takes for us as readers to assimilate it, thus causing us to dwell longer on the image. They add detail not crucial for understanding but crucial for presence. Often in Wolfe these extensions and modifications take place in the middle of the sentence rather than the end, suspending the fulfillment of the main clause and heightening the sense of amplitude.

Abrupt transitions. In the midst of his description of the casino signs, Wolfe shifts, without paragraphing or proleptic phrase, to a portrait of one of the designers:

> Las Vegas' sign makers work so far out beyond the frontiers of conventional studio art that they have no names themselves for the forms they create. Vaughan Cannon, one of those tall, blond Westerners, the builders of places like Las Vegas and Los Angeles, whose eyes seem to have been bleached by the sun, is in the back shop of the Young Electric Sign Company out on East Charleston Boulevard. (8)

The sudden shift after "create" is typical of Wolfe's juxtaposing of tenses, points of view, tones. Several paragraphs later he shifts again, moving from a general observation about the tackiness of Las Vegas fashion to another present tense recreation of a specific scene: "I am in the cocktail lounge of the Hacienda Hotel, talking to managing director Dick Taylor." Longinus associates movement of this sort with passion. "Continuance," he says, "betokens tranquility, while passion—the transport and commotion of the soul—sets order in defiance" (101). Under the pressure of the experience, the writer leaps from subject to subject "as by a veering wind, now this way now that with rapid changes" (103). The running together of sentences and blocks of sentences implies both motion—the rush of the sensory experience being described—and the enthusiasm of the observer in his rush to record it all.

Present tense narration. Notice that part of the shift in these cases involves a shift from past to present tense. "I am in the cocktail lounge . . ."; "I stare, but I am new here"; "Cannon points to where the sign's two great curving faces meet to form a narrow vertical face and says . . ." The strategy here is obviously to give a sense of the experience happening in the now of the essay. "If you introduce things which are past as present and now taking place," Longinus advises, "you will make your story no longer a narration but an actuality" (109–11).

There is more involved here, of course, than just the use of verbs. What makes the scene present is the use of concrete detail and specific observation. To paraphrase Longinus, our impression is that "carried away by enthusiasm and passion," Wolfe thinks he sees what he describes and then places it before the eyes of his readers (83–85). Drawing on Cicero, Quintilian, and the *Rhetorica ad Herennium*, Perelman calls this figure "hypotyposis," a technique of language "which sets things out in such a way that the matter seems to unfold, and the thing to happen, under our eyes" (167). The event is thus not a mere abstraction, an idea fixed on the page and removed from our concerns, but immediate, happening now, in the present of our reading.

Exclamations.   One of the signature devices of Wolfe's style is his periodic bursts of enthusiastic endorsement or identification— "But exactly!" "Of course!" "Just right!" While these interruptions are perhaps too playful and ironic to qualify as expressions of what Longinus calls "vehement and inspired passion," they do imply the intensity of Wolfe's involvement in the actions he is describing. They contribute to the effect of hypotyposis: it's as if Wolfe is reexperiencing his initial enthusiasms in the present of the essay. They also suggest indirectly the power of the event: in the face of the bizarre or the extreme, the writer cannot simply record detail; his own emotional and visceral reactions keep violating the narrative.

Now, for all these strategies and figures we are concerned with the ironic sublime. Longinus would never sanction detailed description of casino signs or female anatomy. But this is just exactly Wolfe's project, to seek out people and experiences without "grandeur" or "stature" and infuse them with enthusiasm, elevating them into objects of aesthetic interest ("New Journalism" 38). The issue is the behavior of language under the pressure of experiences which by definition strain or exceed language. The rhetoric of the sublime provides a useful set of terms for understanding the dynamic of Wolfe's style.

What's important to realize is that Wolfe's prose is intensely figurative, thus intensely rhetorical. Figures, Perelman explains, are "modes of expression which are different from the ordinary" (167). We are struck in our reading of Wolfe by the wealth of his figures. We are made aware of them, made aware of Wolfe in the act of trying to make his language more than ordinary. And this effort, as the context of these passages makes clear, is a response to the inexplicability of Wolfe's object.

Wolfe's language becomes more intense in *Acid Test*. He takes greater risks syntactically and strains harder for complete identification with his subjects. For the most part, he has dropped first person narration in favor of a narrative omniscience which requires him to simulate the drug experience. He tries here to penetrate to the heart of the experience and the consciousness of the participants, and as a result his language assumes a still "freer" form:

> They would take wax pencils, different colors, and scrawl out symbols for each other to improvise on: Sandy the pink drum strokes there, and he would make a sound like *chee-oonh-chunh, chee-oonh-chunh,* and so forth, and Kesey the guitar arrows there, *broinga broinga brang brang,* and Jane Burton the bursts of scat vocals there, and Bob Stone the Voice Over stories to the background of the Human Jazz— all of it recorded on the tape recorder—and then all soaring on— what?—acid, peyote, morning-glory seeds, which were very hell to choke down, billions of bilious seeds mulching out into sodden dandelions in your belly, bloated—but soaring!—or IT-290, or dexedrine, benzedrine, methedrine—Speed!—or speed and grass—sometimes you could take a combination of speed and grass and prop that . . . LSD door open in the mind without going through the whole uncontrollable tumult of the LSD . . . And Sandy takes LSD and the lime :::::: light :::::: and the magical bower turns into . . . *neon dust* . . . pointillist particles for sure, now. Golden particles, brilliant forest-green particles, each one picking up the light, and all shimmering and flowing like an electronic mosaic, pure California neon dust. There is no way to describe how beautiful this discovery is, to actually *see* the atmosphere you have lived in for years for the first time and to feel that it is *inside* of you, too, flowing up from the heart, the torso, into the brain, an electric fountain . . . And . . . IT-290! (60–61)

The passage starts with a balanced, straightfoward declaration of fact, but after the colon the first sentence begins to accelerate. Clauses and phrases are hooked together with successive "ands," as if Wolfe keeps adding new chunks of data or observation as they occur to him, lengthening the sentence with each addition and postponing closure. He is not stopping to refashion the sentence to include the new detail—he adds it on immediately. The sentence and the experience seem simultaneous. The moment is suspended within the confines of the periods, accumulating density and weight each additional instant that closure is postponed. Dashes represent rapid and apparently spontaneous juxtapositions and additions of thought, not carefully subordinated but crammed in at the instant of perception.

The sentence finally ends at "speed and grass" but Wolfe then takes off again, introducing ellipses and double ellipses (or repeated colons) to suggest the speed and simultaneity of his impressions as he recreates or tries to enter into the experience. The ellipsis records a silence, the silence as Wolfe pauses to find the right word, the right phrase. Within the gap we sense the strain of expression—we hear the experience itself as it hovers just beyond the sentence. More "and's" suggest the coordination of unstructured thought. Then there is the sudden and intense juxtaposition of "lime" and "light," just fragmentary bursts of observation hurriedly put down on the page, briefly fixed. Words at this point begin outstripping themselves, the nonlinearity of the moment exceeding the linearity of syntax. Italics magnify the object following an ellipsis (*neon dust*). A fragmentary appositive follows ("Golden particles, brilliant forest-green particles . . ."), restating, repeating, progressively revising what has gone before, and then the appositives are followed by two absolutes ("each one picking up the light," "all shimmering and flowing . . .").

The sentence that extends over these fragments is in effect cumulative—Wolfe begins the sentence with a main clause expressing the essential concept, then adds participials, appositives, absolutes, or relative clauses which progressively refine and revise that concept. He could end the sentence after the initial declarative sentence, but instead he continues the thought, as if further dimensions of the concept have occurred to him in the process of writing the main clause, as if he hasn't gotten the image right the first time, hasn't adequately described all there is to describe and must keep searching for the right phrase. Rather than presenting the idea in a balanced simile, its configurations thought out and established in advance, the sentence grows and develops organically, each phrase or clause suggesting the one that follows.

In the next sentence Wolfe emerges from this syntactic chaos to make it clear that the experience he is struggling to express is in fact difficult if not impossible to put into words. He then returns to exclamations and fragments. There is the ellipsis—his pausing to think, his recording of the act of composing—then another "and," then, without transition or explanation or even grammatical apparatus, the shouting of the name itself: "IT-290!"

In "The New Journalism," Wolfe explains that exclamation points, italics, and abrupt shifts help him give the illusion in his writing "not only of a person talking but of a person thinking" (22). In the terms we have been developing, we would say that the passage is an example of hypotypotic development. It tries to give the illusion of events taking place before the eyes of the reader— and not only the events themselves, but the describing of the events. Or perhaps all this can be seen as an example of what Longinus calls "hyperbata," or "departures in the order of expressions or ideas from the natural sequence." When moved by passion, we slip excitedly from word to word, "foisting in the midst some irrelevant matter, and then again wheel around" to the original theme (103). If "continuance betokens tranquility," then stream-of-consciousness betokens intensity. Whatever the specific terminology, there is a crucial link between the magnitude of the experience and a spontaneity of composition. Under the pressure of the sublime—or of any intense, difficult to describe experience—"the words issue forth without connecting links and are poured out as it were, almost outstripping the speaker himself" (99). The language is "not premeditated," but "prompted by the necessity of the moment" (105). Indeed, this is exactly how Wolfe himself describes his first use of the freer forms of the New Journalism. Unable to express his subject in any conventional form, he just started typing the notes out as a memorandum. "I just started recording it all," he says, "typing along like a madman" (xiii). In the face of the experience, he forgot the constraints of linear and publically acceptable journalism. He developed the technique of using "anything that came into my head," as he puts it in "The New Journalism," much of it "thrown together in a rough and awkward way" (15).

The passage also illustrates Wolfe's technique of suddenly entering into the mind of a character and adopting that character's language: " 'Too much!' says George, because, of course he knows—all of us sliding in and out of these combinations of mutual consciousness, intersubjectivity. . . . [ellipsis mine] One of us finds a bunch of wooden chessmen. They are carved figures" (61). This is not Wolfe speaking in his own voice. Chameleon-like, he has assumed the language and style of the pranksters, and without the signposts of quotation marks and paragraphing to indicate the shift. In fact, throughout the passage it is never clear how much of what Wolfe is saying is in his own voice and how much is refashioned from his extensive saturation-reporting interviews with the individuals involved. His technique is to "shift as quickly as possible into the eye sockets, as it were, of the people in the story," even to "shift the point of view in the middle of a paragraph or even a sentence" (18).

As Longinus puts it, "there is further the case in which a writer, when relating something about a person, suddenly breaks off and converts himself into that self-same person." This species of figure, he says, "is a kind of outburst of passion" (113). In his involvement with his characters, Wolfe gives the impression of being carried away into a complete identification. The result is presence. We are inside the character. It is not just Wolfe's own impressions that are spontaneously arranging themselves on the page; in the end he has come to share in the stream-of-consciousness of the people he is describing.

The Right Stuff is more controlled syntactically than *Acid Test* and more detached tonally. Perhaps the reserve of the fighter jocks influences Wolfe's style here. Yet he still draws on the strategies of sublimity and presence we have been tracing. His attempt to describe the right stuff itself is perhaps the best example of how he must intensify his rhetorical machinery to approximate the intensity and quality of his inexplicable, privileged object. We see him here, clearly in the presence of experiences which defy more than provisional formulation, pushing against the envelope of language.

The right stuff cannot be explained rationally or even satisfactorily defined. But the term itself can be repeated, over and over again, almost as a refrain: "the elected and annointed ones who had *the right stuff*," "those men who had the right stuff," "the arena of the right stuff," "*left behind* for lack of the right stuff," "the pyramid of the right stuff," "the altar of the right stuff" (24–25). The phrase comes to dominate our attention over the course of the chapter; with each rephrasing it glows brighter, sounds louder. Notice, too, that along with many other terms and phrases in this section, it is frequently italicized, a visual indication that it is meant to be read as louder or more emphatic. Wolfe takes a word as it is in itself and then through manuscript devices or simple repetition tries to enlarge it in our minds, make us notice it more ("I tried to yell right in his ear," he says in "The New Journalism," "Stick around!" [15]).

Wolfe creates presence, too, by using the insider's language of the fighter jocks. The section as a whole is grounded in the expository language of Wolfe as outside evaluator and analyst, but within his explanations he often shifts into the jargon of the pilots themselves—converting himself into the self-same person, as it were, shifting into their eye sockets: "*That shape!—It's so damned small!*" or "Provided you have the right stuff, you miserable pudknocker" (26, 37). The effect is to recreate the experience, dramatizing it rather than simply interpreting it.

Part of this shift in point of view or voice involves, too, a shift from analysis to concrete narration. Suddenly, within a paragraph, we are brought down on the deck of a heaving aircraft carrier:

> It *heaved,* it moved up and down underneath his feet, it pitched up, it pitched down, it rolled to port (this great beast *rolled!*) and it rolled to starboard, as the ship moved into the wind and, therefore, into the waves, and the wind kept sweeping across, sixty feet up in the air out in the open sea, and there were no railings whatsoever. This was a *skillet!*—a frying pan!—a short-order grill!—not gray but black, smeared with skid marks from one end to the other and glistening

with pools of hydraulic fluid and the occasional jet-fuel slick, all of it still hot, sticky, greasy, runny, virulent from God knows what traumas—still ablaze!—consumed in detonations, explosions, flames, combustion, roars, shrieks, whines, blasts, horrible shudders, fracturing impacts, as little men in screaming red and yellow and purple and green shirts with black Mickey Mouse helmets over their ears skittered about on the surface as if for their very lives (you've said it now!) hooking fighter planes onto the catapult shuttles so that they can explode their afterburners and be slung off the deck in a red-mad fury with a *kaboom!* that pounds through the entire deck. (26–27)

Coming, as it does, after Wolfe's claim that the experience of landing on a aircraft carrier cannot be rendered in words, this remarkable description is somewhat ironic. He has made the moment happen on the page. He has worked himself into such a state that he thinks he sees what he describes, as if he is there now, and in the process he places it before the eyes of the readers. The sentences accumulate, phrases and clauses and parenthetical interjections extending the main clause, dashes marking juxtapositions and shifts in focus. His point of view subtly mixes the voice of the outside observer ("therefore") with the voice of the participants ("this great beast rolled!"). Italics and exclamations magnify phrases. A wry undertone suggests both the humor and the danger of the situation ("you've said it now!"). The passage as a whole accelerates, climaxes, crescendos, intensifies, then intensifies again, and all the while Wolfe seems to revel in his own energy.

An important part of this passage—and an important part of Wolfe's style throughout his writing—is what we might call the evocation of surrounding scenic detail or the evocation of the scenic frame. Wolfe's effort is to pick the significant detail from a complex landscape or scene, the detail that when detached from its context will in itself evoke the context. He looks for the phrase or image from the welter of experience which will most resonate, suggesting by association a matrix of other details. What's interesting is that these details are not in themselves necessarily or directly connected to the central idea or impression Wolfe is trying to evoke. They are usually peripheral. But Wolfe realizes that peripheral detail, the "off-camera material," has a way of implying the central event. The writer tries not to describe the scene directly—overly detailed descriptions would defeat purpose—but to jog the reader's memory. One detail can trigger a whole complex of memories not stated—the "reader's memory (if any) . . . is invited to fill in the rest" ("New Journalism" 48).

Here the random off-camera details are the Mickey Mouse ears and brightly colored shirts of the men who guide the planes onto the carrier, or the hot, sticky, greasy fluid that glistens on the carrier surface. In a later description in this same chapter Wolfe describes the sight of the sun "just beginning to cook up behind the rim of the horizon" and the "little red light on top of the water towers" as the pilot gets ready to take off in "the chilly light of dawn" (38). These are details of the frame, not of the picture. They evoke the scene of the drama, not the drama itself—not the action of the pilots, their interior consciousness, above all, not what it actually feels like to have the right stuff. There is no necessary relationship between the little red light on top of the water towers and the experience of bravery or mastery. The details are metonymies, not synecdoches. And yet there is something in these contextual impressions which carries with it an implicit sense of much broader feelings and meanings. As Wolfe explains in "The New Journalism," the apparently random details that come to be a part of a people's "status life" are not mere "embroidery" but something at the "center" (32).

For all these reasons Wolfe's style is effective. What I earlier called his "rhetorical virtuosity"—his mastery of figures, sentence rhythms, and concrete detail—makes experience present on the page, present in our minds as readers. At the boundaries of expression, under the pressures of the inexplicable, the vast, the grand—what I have wanted to see as in some ways the sublime—he achieves power. There is a real sense in *The Right Stuff* in which Wolfe is clearly competing with the astronauts on the level of language, matching their stunts and "hassling" and fly-overs with hypotyposis, amplification, hyperbata. The sublimity of the experience draws out this kind of language, calls it forth; it is a response to the intensity of the moment. And in its intensity, its rhetorical variety, it comes close to the threshold of these finally impenetrable experiences.

There is another important sense in which Wolfe "succeeds" as a writer even in the face of the inexplicable. The experiences he sets out to describe in *Streamline Baby*, *Acid Test*, and *The Right Stuff* are fundamentally experiential: they can't be explained, only experienced; discursive formulations or analysis miss the texture and the feel of the moment. All the strategies of presence we have been examining help to evoke that presence. The language is experiential, as opposed to logical. "I have tried," Wolfe says at the end of *Acid Test*, "not only to tell what the Pranksters did but to recreate the mental atmosphere or subjective reality of it. I don't think their adventure can be understood without that" (415). Wolfe's subject cannot be understood in the abstract. To accomplish his end—to inform us about this culture, this life, make it present to us, make us aware of it—he turns to scene-by-scene reconstruction and all the rhetorical strategies available to a writer for fixing impressions in the consciousness of the reader. He doesn't explain, he dramatizes, and for that reason we do come in the end to understand something of the subjective reality of the pranksters and the fighter jocks.

III

But there is also an important sense in which these strategies of apparent presence suggest an absence. In the end Wolfe's style does not depend on imitative form but on a disjunction between form and subject.

The ellipses we have seen do more than suggest spontaneity of composition. What they dramatize is Wolfe in the act of trying to discover the right word—more particularly, that moment in the act of composition when Wolfe must pause, search, strain, reach for a word that finally isn't there. "As to just what this ineffable quality was . . . well, it obviously involved bravery" or "And yet once the newcomer's two feet were on it . . . *Geometry*—my God, man, this is a . . . skillet!"—language momentarily breaks down in the space that opens up between "was" and "well," "it" and "geometry," and even though there is something a bit staged in this maneuver, something a bit too consciously dramatized, the impression is struggle. By recreating the experience of spontaneous composition, Wolfe has chosen to reveal those moments when the stream of consciousness is interrupted by the ineffable.

The loosening and abandoning of syntactic or grammatical order also testifies to the breakdown of language in the passages we have looked at so far. Wolfe's sentences decay into fragments which are then juxtaposed without linear sequence. The absence of predicates or connecting phrases shows the disintegration of words in the face of the sublime. A short passage from *Acid Test* nicely dramatizes this particular tension:

> —and none of them would have understood it, anyway, even if someone had told them what was happening. Kesey had already bought a new place in La Honda, California. He had already proposed to a dozen people on the Lane that they come with him, move the whole scene, the whole raggedy-manic Era, off to . . . Versailles, his Low Rent Versailles, over the mountain and through the woods, in La Honda, Calif. Where—where—in the lime ::::::: light :::::: and the neon dust—
> ". . . a considerable new message . . . the blissful counterstoke . . ." (55)

First the statement that the experience is inexplicable, then the move into this deliberately fragmentary language—the missing predicates, the juxtaposition of "where's," the stuttering in effect, the double ellipses. The experience will not submit to the linear ordering of language; language fails here. It does not make sense. It reflects the fact that the prankster experience does not make sense. Wolfe is simply echoing the pranksters' language at this point, which consists by and large of obscure metaphorical allusions, repeated code words, and significant silences. It is often violently meaningless, a perverse mantra. Language is not adequate for describing the nature of their private vision.

From the beginning Wolfe's material defies formulation, and the forms his writing takes are in a very real sense a result of failure. "At first I couldn't even write the story," he says of his experience with "The Kandy-Kolored Tangerine-Flake Streamline Baby." He "had a lot of trouble analyzing exactly what [he] had on his hands"; the material was too "weird," too "nutty" and "crazy." It's only after telling his editor that he simply "couldn't pull the thing together" that he discovers the "freer forms" of the New Journalism, and these forms involve the abandoning of form, the decision to "just start recording it all," "typing along like a madman" without regard for the final shape of the piece or its internal logic (xii). Even though it ultimately assumes a logic and power of its own, the new style of "Streamline Baby" is an antistyle, a response to the inability of language to capture the experience.

All the strategies of presence are a substitute for strategies of proof or analysis. For Perelman presence is opposed to "rationalistic" forms of presentation. Longinus contrasts the figures of sublimity with figures of "proof." While logical strategies of inference and documentation "demonstrate the matter under investigation," the strategies of sublimity or presence "lend strength to the argument by dwelling upon it" (77). Presence does not advance the theme. It does not explain it, adding new and distinct ideas or supporting documentation or logical analysis. Ultimately it simply repeats or amplifies the notion, particularizing it, making it a part of a rhythmic pattern which keeps the statement or idea itself in the foreground of our consciousness. It magnifies rather than analyzes.

Repetition itself, the most basic strategy of presence, is a good example of this limitation. In repeating the phrase "the right stuff" over and over in the central chapter of the book, Wolfe is acting out his inability to define it. He cannot tell us what it us, only that it is. He cannot explain it to us, only make us increasingly aware of it as a phrase with its own power or persuasiveness. To put this in terms of argumentation, he cannot give us any warrants for accepting the proposition; he can only state the proposition itself over and over in different forms. Unable to extend the phrase, he repeats it. In the essay on Las Vegas he devotes the entire opening paragraph simply to repeating "Hernia" (3–4). It is a nonsense word, nothing more than the droning chant of a man at the craps table, and repeated dozens of times over the course of a paragraph it comes to emphasize the breakdown of language amidst the sensory overload of the casino. It demonstrates in an exaggerated way the suggestion of meaninglessness or inexplicability implicit in all of Wolfe's repetitions.

Select details can trigger complexes of memory and association. But in a key statement in "The New Journalism," Wolfe acknowledges that some experiences are difficult to evoke in this way because the reader has no associations to call on, as for example in an LSD experience (47–48). The use of triggering detail depends on the active participation of the reader; the words themselves do not accomplish the act of communication. If the reader has no experiences to relate to the words—or is unwilling to do the relating—the language fails. The use of detail involves indirection by its nature.

Wolfe explains the problem quite explicitly in *The Right Stuff*:

> To talk about it in so many words was forbidden, of course. The very words *death, danger, bravery, fear* were not to be uttered except in the occasional specific instance or for ironic effect. Nevertheless, the subject could be adumbrated in *code* or *by example*. Hence the endless evenings of pilots huddled together talking about flying. On these long and drunken evenings (the bane of family life) certain theorems would be propounded and demonstrated—and all by *code* and *example*. (34)

The response to the inexplicability of the experience of flying—or to the manly taboo about the expression of feeling—is code and example, concrete embodiments of ideas which do not explicitly state those ideas. An example does not explicate itself; it implies its meaning or application. In relying on stories the astronauts can point to their meaning without violating the code of silence. They know that their audience will supply the corresponding interpretation for every concrete clue. They count on the participation of the listener.

There is, then, a crucial absence, recognized as an absence, in the use of concrete detail: codes and examples do not mean what they say. What's missing is an explicit "theorem" or interpretative formulation of the experience. The use of codes and examples is an acknowledgment that such direct formulations are impossible, for whatever reasons. They testify to the failure of explicit statement. What can't be formulated can only be hinted at.

Furthermore, if, as Wolfe suggests in "The New Journalism," the reader does not have appropriate associations to supply himself, the problem is even more vexing. Codes and examples work indirectly, and in this case the paths of indirection are cut off. As readers we are not fighter jocks. We cannot follow the instructions for comparing and intepreting left by the concrete clues of codes and examples.

Of course, Wolfe is describing here his own necessary method as an expositor in *The Right Stuff*. His method is to provide example after example of what the right stuff is in lieu of some kind of explicit abstract definition. Each concrete illustration is in a sense simply a repetition rather than an extension of the unstateable thesis, a particularized reformulation rather than an explanation. In using the insider's slang of the fighter jocks, Wolfe tries to adopt their code. He cannot explain the right stuff to us but he can use the language which the pilots use to imply it to each other. He can sound as if he has had the experience himself.

In the end what we have is the frame of the picture, not the picture itself. Kesey ridicules the "White Smocks" who conducted the Stanford LSD experiments because they failed to understand this distinction. You can "give them a good case of an ashtray turning into a Venus flytrap or eyelid movies of crystal cathedrals," but "visual stuff was just the decor with LSD." The sensory details—and this clearly has implications for everything that Wolfe is trying to accomplish as a writer—evoke the landscape of the action, not the action itself; the stage, not the drama. "The whole thing was . . . *the experience* . . . this certain indescribable *feeling*," and this feeling is not necessarily related to the landscape in which it occurs. Its relationship to surface detail is only metonymic, not synecdochic. "Words can only jog the memory," Wolfe continues in Kesey's voice, "and if there is no memory of . . . The *Experience*—" (46). The experience Wolfe is trying to penetrate is fundamentally internal and conceptual, even abstract, we might say. The sensory detail can only "jog" (to return to that word from "The New Journalism") the reader's sense of that inner feeling, and because the bonds between the externals and the feeling are so tenuous, that jogging is not reliable, particularly for outsiders, since they have not actually shared in the experience and thus have no even tenuous associations to do the jogging.

Wolfe's explicit commentary on the inexplicability of the experiences he is trying to describe is also a strategy for calling our attention to the struggle of expression and ultimately to the failure of language. In comparing the pranksters' experience to mysticism or the advancement of fighter jocks to Calvinistic election, in repeatedly insisting that the experience of LSD or spaceflight is private, privileged, difficult if not impossible for an outsider to appreciate, Wolfe is acknowledging and then heightening a tension in his language. Such "metadiscourse," such discourse about discoursing, indicates a displacement. He may not be able to describe what it actually feels like to take LSD or pilot a fighter jet, but he can tell us what it feels like to try to describe those sensations. Though Wolfe cannot actually present the experience, he can write *about* it. The underlying drama becomes the story of the writing of the text.

IV

There is a way of recovering from this apparent failure and claiming these tensions for rhetorical ends. In the logic of the sublime, the very failure of imagination to encompass the object of the experience testifies to the grandeur and magnitude of that object. This is implicit in Longinus but worked out fully only in the eighteenth century in Edmund Burke and Immanuel Kant. It is the negative logic underlying the success of the fragment as a literary form in romanticism. For Longinus language seems to buckle and break under the pressure of the sublime, violating its natural order, shifting from idea to idea rapidly and without transition, sometimes literally trailing off into silences which indicate the inability of the speaker to continue. Yet for him it is precisely these deviations in language which become figurative. These apparent breakdowns are what create sublimity in a discourse.

Kant explains the psychology of the effect in *The Critique of Judgment*. In the sublime moment, he says, the mind is overwhelmed by what at first appears to be something "absolutely great" or powerful in nature. The imagination fails to grasp the magnitude or dynamism of the object, striving futilely to represent to the mind the totality of the event. But Kant goes on to suggest that in this very breakdown of representation the mind comes to sense its "supersensible destination" (108). The failure of imagination suggests the value and intensity of the sublime object. The failure to signify signifies.

Wolfe clearly has this in mind in his analysis of the hysteria that followed the first Russian manned spaceflights. What inflamed the public imagination was the mysteriousness of the Russian space program. No one knew who was behind the successes; no one knew in advance when they were to happen; no one knew exactly how the Russians proceeded. In the absence of knowledge, the program assumed mythical proportions. Wolfe clearly has this in mind in his analysis of the fighter jock's ironic understatement, what he calls the phenomenon of "pygmalion in reverse." There is, he says, an inverse proportion between the icy calmness of the pilot's language and the danger he is actually facing. The calmer, the cooler, the more understated the description coming from the cockpit, the greater the danger. In a slightly different way this is the rhetorical principle at work in the pranksters' "groking" over Kesey's oracular, apparently nonsensical pronouncements. The very fragmentariness and disjointedness of these aphorisms is an index to their profundity. The failure to signify signifies.

We can also appreciate the irony at work here in terms of what Perelman calls "the argument by sacrifice," a "quasi-logical form of measurement" (252). If we are willing to sacrifice money, time, or even our lives for a cause, we indicate the worth of that cause in our view. The greater the sacrifice, the greater the implicit value of the object. We evaluate one term by the other. In the same way the effort which Wolfe expends in pursuit of the right stuff or the Unspoken Thing is an index of the worth of those subjects. If the subject is difficult to express—if Wolfe must "sacrifice" to bring it to the page—it has value.

The irony is all the greater if the writer making the sacrifice is talented. If I, with my great ability to use words and render experiences vividly and convincingly in language, am unable to express this particular concept, how great must this concept be? And (the irony cutting both ways), if I am able even to approximate expression of this great object or concept, how talented must I be?

I am edging up here on the problem of claiming that failures can be successes in language. In what way is Wolfe ironic at these junctures? Is he really suggesting that his object is inexplicable, or is he creating this tension in the prose to aggrandize his own ability, creating a standard against which to measure his powers of description? Or, avoiding now the problem of determining intentions, if the dramatization of the failure of expression is in fact a figure for making experience present, if absence can lead to presence, how acute is the problem of inexplicability?

It seems to me that the very success of Wolfe's language ultimately recasts the problem of expression we have been concerned with. The fact that his supposed failures are clearly figurative leads to the same problem on a different level.

Wolfe's style is "foregrounded," to borrow a term that Tony Tanner uses to describe the style of much American literature, from Melville to James, and which he in turn, interestingly, borrows from G. B. Tennyson's study of Carlyle's *Sartor Resartus*. Wolfe "use[s] language in such a way that it draws attention to itself" (*City of Words* 20). Reading Wolfe we are aware of his figurative stunts, his swoops and dives and repetitions of structures, his reworking of the devices of punctuation. His style is *figurative*: based on a series of deviations from the norms of language which as deviations call attention to themselves. His "verbal display," as Tanner would put it, his "visible verbal performance," invites us to "linger at the surface" of the language (20).

Typography alone emphasizes textuality. When Wolfe violates the boundaries of the paragraph, opening up the margins of the text, we do not get a sense of the experience he is trying to imitate but more a sense of the words themselves in their spatial arrangement on the page:

Miles

    Miles

        Miles

            Miles

                Miles

                    Miles

                        Miles

                                under all that good

vegetation from Morris Orchids and having visions of

Faces

    Faces

        Faces

            Faces

                Faces

                    Faces

                      Faces

                                so many faces rolling up

behind the eyelids, faces he has never seen before. (*Acid Test* 48–49)

Wolfe is obviously trying to convey the impression of nonlinearity or simultaneity of experience. He wants us to see that the experience exceeds the boundaries of the sentence. Yet the effect is to emphasize that Wolfe is rearranging the words on the page. What we see is not the experience but the unusual order of the sentence. We see blank space, not the illusion of the reality. In the act of imitation, Wolfe has violated presence.

Double ellipses, repeated exclamation points, italics and all the manuscript devices for magnifying presence have the same effect. They call attention to themselves. While they are meant to convey emotion and intensity—to correspond as language to the intensity of the experience and thus to make us share in that intensity—they in fact remind us that we are reading words, deciphering black marks on a white background.

With crucial exceptions, Wolfe, like Capote, maintains what in the next chapter I will call a narrative "silence," inhabiting the minds of his characters and recreating their experience rather than commenting in his own person. Yet even more than Capote, he is present in the very style of his prose. His amplifications and repetitions and piling up of figures are more than traces of his voice. Reading him we say, here is Wolfe amplifying, repeating, piling up figures, pushing language to its limits. The visceral illusion of actually having the experience is never fully maintained in Wolfe. We never forget that we are participating in a verbal performance. We never forget Wolfe. He may push against the outside of the envelope, but he always remains inside.

Wolfe is trapped within language on another level as well. In "The New Journalism" he prides himself on "scene-by-scene reconstruction," his ability to tell a story "by moving from scene to scene and resorting as little as possible to sheer historical narrative" (31). But in practice Wolfe doesn't always show. He often tells, often resorts to historical narrative. It is partly a problem of lyric intensity. He can sustain moments of reconstruction or hypotypotic recreation only briefly. Concrete descriptions lose their interest and force over the course of a long retelling. If not for pacing, at least a thread of narrative commentary is necessary to hold the scenes together.

But more than that, it is in the voice of the expositor that Wolfe most reveals himself. It is as expositor that he gives shape and significance to his material. We have been considering this voice from the beginning, since it is as expositor that Wolfe analyzes the problem of inexplicability, identifying his subject as beyond language and then following out the implications of that problem. What we need to see now is that this voice has rhetorical consequences of its own.

In his comparison of the pranksters to religious groups, Wolfe adopts a middle style somewhere between the pranksters' own language and the language of Joachim Wach, Max Weber and the other scholars he quotes for his analysis. Wach's style is stolid and academic: "Following a profound new experience, providing a new illumination of the world, the founder, a highly charismatic person, begins enlisting disciples." Wolfe's analytical voice, in contrast, is both more concrete and more enthusiastic: "What they all saw in . . . a flash was the solution to the basic predicament of being *human*, the personal *I*, *Me*, trapped, mortal and helpless, in a vast impersonal *It*, the world around me. Suddenly!—All in one!—flowing together" (129). But while Wolfe's language is not as rigid or formal as Wach's, mixing the academic and the enthusiastic, it is still analytical. It still seeks to explain and understand. It still generalizes, abstracts, interprets. The pranksters, he says, develop their own symbols, terminology, life styles. Simple cultic practices grow out of the new experience. As Wach himself points out, at this juncture the group develops an urge to extend the message to other people—and so on.

We can't dismiss this section of analysis as the expression of one voice among the many Wolfe mimics. The entire chapter "The Unspoken Thing" comes after a long stretch of scene-by-scene reconstruction where Wolfe has not emerged directly at all in his own voice. His emergence here signals something important. Moreover, the analysis of the inexplicability of the experience brings together and clarifies a theme that has been implicit from the beginning. It is Wolfe's attempt to step back and explain the meaning of the experience he has been recreating.

The chapter "The Right Stuff" comes at roughly the same point in that book and for roughly the same reasons of pacing. From the beginning Wolfe has recreated the experience scene by scene, not commenting in his own person, and now he steps back to explore the implications of those stories and examples. He has repeatedly referred to the "right stuff"; it has become a refrain in his narrative. Now he pauses to explain more directly what it means. This shift from the particular to the general, from reconstruction to exposition, signals the importance of the chapter. The language is now pitched higher.

And now Wolfe's style has changed. He is no longer trying to speak in the voice of the participants. He is no longer an insider. Instead he assumes the role of the outside observer abstracting and analyzing. It is a mixed style, carrying traces of the experiential language of the first third of the book. Wolfe easily slips into the voices of his characters, and rhythmically his sentences still have the same amplifying structures and emphasis. But it is clear that Wolfe is now trying to explain and define the right stuff, not dramatize it: "Perhaps because it could not be talked about, the subject began to take on superstitious and even mystical outlines. A man either had it or he didn't. There was no such thing as having most if it. Moreover, it could blow at any seam." Or, "There was something ancient, primordial, irresistible about the challenge of this stuff, no matter what a sophisticated and rational age one might think he lived in" (29). There is more than a little irony here in the disjunction between Wolfe's observations about the "primordial" quality of the right stuff and his use of words like "primordial." This is an abstract, rational, analytical language which is at odds with the experience it is interpreting.

Wolfe does not completely conform to the experience. He is not entirely a chameleon adopting the jargon of the insiders. His language fails at mimesis even where it succeeds at analysis. It is much different than conventional prose, much closer to the shape and texture of the experiences it describes, but in the end it is still a shaping, conservative kind of language, an effort to interpret, understand, reflecting the sensibilities of an educated outsider, a bearer of language.

After all, Wolfe is describing the right stuff, putting it into so many words. He is doing what no fighter jock would ever do. By virtue of the fact that he is writing a book, in whatever form, at whatever level of sympathy and engagement, he is an outsider. In

Kesey's view, the experience of LSD is antithetical to any kind of linear order. "Any attempt to plan, compose, orchestrate, write a script," Wolfe explains, "only locked you out of the moment, back in the world of conditioning and training where the brain was a reducing valve" (60). In his expository voice Wolfe plans, composes, orchestrates, his language a reducing valve. I have said that in his moments of scene-by-scene reconstruction Wolfe implies that the inexplicable feeling or experience can never be formulated discursively or analytically. It does not lend itself to abstract statement. But as expositor Wolfe does abstract and then formulate statements about this ineffable quality. He does define it, speak it.

As scene-by-scene reconstructor, then, Wolfe uses a foregrounded style which calls attention to itself and thus makes him an outsider to the experience. As expositor, he uses an ordering, analytical language which makes him an outsider. This is the controlling tension throughout Wolfe's work, a tension that he continually features and highlights. As Tanner says of Melville, Hawthorne, James and others in the central American literary tradition, Wolfe is sensitive to the power and the limitations of language. He is linguistically self-conscious. And given this self-consciousness, form *qua* form in Wolfe has rhetorical and thematic consequences of great importance. Explicitly, in narrative commentary, or implicitly, in the very act of creating a style, Wolfe calls our attention to the envelope of language. In the end, it is his very effort to push against the outside of that envelope that traps him inside.

V

Or to put this another way, despite his effort to rupture the membrane of language, to accommodate new extraverbal and nonverbal experiences, in the end Wolfe remains inside the envelope and in fact defends, argues for the envelope. In the end he is on the side of language. Wolfe is not finally trapped at all. Rather, his implicit argument is that language must prevail against the nonverbal and extraverbal. His social criticism is acted out in the very writing of his books, in his acts of ordering, wording, interpreting and recreating.

Wolfe's narrative detachment makes it somewhat difficult to know whose side he is on. Because he proceeds by scene-by-scene reconstruction rather than by explicit commentary, his sympathies are not easy to determine. He ostensibly seeks to inform rather than deliberate, engaging in "reportage" rather than "inference," to return to Weaver's terms.

On the one hand his sympathy for the pranksters and the test pilots is implicit in the very effort to push the outside of the envelope. The energy and enthusiasm of his language as he attempts to capture the experiences of these closed fraternities in itself signals his endorsement. In his ability to recreate scenes through the eye sockets of the participants, we become participants as readers and thus inevitably come to sympathize with the point of view we inhabit.

In *Acid Test* Wolfe starts out frankly admitting his skepticism about the pranksters. An "I" is present in the opening pages, the "I" of the hardheaded East Coast journalist resistant to radical scams. But almost immediately Wolfe finds himself drawn into the experience. "It's phony, goddam it," he says of their oracular conversations, "but *mysto* . . . and after a while it starts to infect you, like an itch, the roseola" (21). And he says several scenes later, ' Despite the skepticism I brought here, *I* am suddenly experiencing *their* feeling. I am sure of it. I feel like I am in on something the outside world I came from could not possibly comprehend" (29). Soon the "I" of the outside observer vanishes and Wolfe is inside the characters, sharing their perceptions of the world.

Like the test pilots or the California customizers, Kesey is a figure of imagination. He represents the claims of the transcendent and the uninhibited over and against the stultifying restrictions of middle-class life. Wolfe's fascination with select groups of gifted or exceptional people and his preoccupation with experiences on the "edge" should be seen in direct opposition to the conventional bourgeois mores we can assume obtain for most of his readers. The "true mystic brotherhood" of the pranksters is for Wolfe a commentary on "poor old Formica polyethylene 1960s America," the "marshmallow shiny black shoe masses" (31–32). Kesey's critiques of the Young Turks, the Berkeley radical intelligensia, and the La Honda middle class are to a large extent Wolfe's own: "The Youth had always had only three options: go to school, get a job or live at home. And—how boring each was!—compared to the experience of . . . the infinite . . . and a life in which the subject is not scholastic or bureaucratic but . . . *Me* and *Us*." Wolfe's interests are clearly with the "*attuned* ones amid the non-musical shiny-black-shoe multitudes" (66).

In *The Right Stuff* the attuned ones amid the multitudes are the test pilots, individuals literally and figuratively above the rest of us:

> From *up here* at dawn the pilot looked down upon poor hopeless Las Vegas (or Yuma, Corpus Christi, Meridian, San Berandino, or Dayton) and began to wonder: How can all of them down there, those poor souls who will soon be waking up and trudging out of their minute rectangles and inching along their little noodle highways toward whatever slots and grooves make up their everyday lives—how could they live like that, with such earnestness, if they had the faintest idea of what it was like up here in this righteous zone? (38–39)

Wolfe's sympathies are with the pilots in this passage. Their flying is a metaphor for his desire to transcend the minute rectangles and the slots and grooves that make up everyday lives. His rhetorical project can be seen as the effort to lift us out of that mundane existence by enabling us to experience in some provisional way this sense of transcendence and privilege.

Wolfe's famous attack on the "beige" style of conventional journalism makes his sympathies still more obvious. The "calm, cultivated and, in fact, genteel" narrator of traditional reporting is a "bore," a "pedestrian mind, a phlegmatic spirit, a faded personality . . . a pallid little troll"—in short, the stylistic equivalent of the marshmallow faces of the black shoe masses exploding in disbelief as the pranksters race by on the bus (17). Wolfe's New Journalism correponds to the subversive and radical values of the pranksters or the masculine charisma of the test pilots: "personality, energy, drive, bravura . . . style, in a word" (18).

But this is just the point. Wolfe's interest in the pranksters or the astronauts is stylistic. He doesn't want to follow them into the silences of pure experience but rather to claim them for style.

Wolfe cannot be on the side of the figures he describes because they represent in the end the nonverbal and the antiverbal.

There are other indications that Wolfe cannot totally sympathize with Kesey. As the experience with the pranksters develops, energies flag and hypocrisies begin to show. Kesey is both the prankster and "the Organizer," a manipulator of his friends. Gradually he appears selfish and egotistical, if not demented. In an important monologue towards the end of the book, Wolfe reveals Kesey's paranoia about the police in Mexico. The crazed, stream-of-consciousness narrative here shows Kesey to be an insecure and ridiculous fool (287ff.). By the time the final acid tests are taking place, Wolfe has resumed his role as reporter, relaying interviews with participants as an observing "I." Significantly, he does not participate himself in the LSD experiments. In the end, in the final graduation beyond drugs, Kesey is a somewhat pathetic, burnt-out prophet unable to organize the epiphany.

Even in Wolfe's most ecstatic celebrations of intensity, the subtle connotations of his words distort the presentation, interposing a layer of irony:

> As to just what this ineffable quality was . . . well, it obviously involved bravery. But it was not bravery in the simple sense of being willing to risk your life. The idea seemed to be that any fool could do that, if that was all that was required, just as any fool could throw away his life in the process. No, the idea here (in the all-enclosing fraternity) seemed to be that a man should have the ability to go up in a hurtling piece of machinery and put his hide on the line and then have the moxie, the reflexes, the experience, the coolness, to pull it back in the last yawning moment—and then to go up again *the next day,* and the next day, and every next day, even if the series should prove infinite—and, ultimately, in its best expression, do so in a cause that means something to thousands, to a people, a nation, to humanity, to God. (*Right Stuff* 24)

Wolfe's great ability as a stylist is to celebrate and satirize his subject at the same time. It is easy to detect the enthusiasm of this passage. But at the same time the description is perceptibly distorted by the informal, almost off-hand rhythms, the italicized expression, the parentheses, all of which imply that Wolfe is imitating voices he does not wholly endorse. The final series—to thousands, to a people, a nation, to humanity, to God—is a deliberatly melodramatic heightening, both playful and ironic. Wolfe is a bit like the consummate actor winking at us in the middle of a passionate scene.

But the real irony is the style itself. It is difficult to believe that Wolfe can wholeheartedly share the pranksters' rejection of order, meaning, and language when the language he uses to describe the pranksters is nuanced, subtle, layered, figurative. The frame qualifies the picture. We have been considering the foregroundedness of Wolfe's style as an indication of his failure, but it is possible to view it positively as an implicit signal of his final interpretation of the experience. His metadiscursiveness sets us up for this irony. Because Wolfe has repeatedly called our attention to the linguistic dimensions of his subject, because he has continually emphasized that Kesey and the astronauts represent realms of inexplicable experience, the densely textured and figurative quality of his language comes to signify his allegiance to language and his identity as a writer. When the issue is defined as a tension between words and silence, any use of language will be rhetorically significant. When that language is flamboyant and foregrounded and intensely figurative, the implications for theme are even stronger.

This is not to downplay the powerful ambiguity in Wolfe's stance. He is both attracted and repelled by the righteous and nonverbal insiders of his books. His language strains and expands and pushes to approximate the quality of the inexplicable and sublime object. But in the end it is language. In "The New Journalism" Wolfe describes himself arriving in New York in the early sixties:

> I couldn't believe the scene I saw spread out before me. New York was pandemonium with a big grin on. . . . [ellipsis mine] It was a hulking carnival. But what really amazed me was that as a writer I had it practically all to myself. As fast as I could possibly do it, I was turning out articles on this amazing spectacle that I saw bubbling and screaming right there in front of my wondering eyes—New York!—and all the while I just knew that some enterprising novelist was going to come

along and *do* this whole marvelous scene with one gigantic daring bold stroke. It was so ready, so *ripe*—so beckoning . . . but it never happened. To my great amazement New York simply remained the journalist's bonzana. (30)

This is not radical Kesey abandoning the novel for nihilistic cross-country movie making. It is not a mumbling Yeager withholding feeling in the code of the manly, single combat warrior. It is certainly not the artist straining to escape language. Wolfe wants to *do* New York and the whole sublime, American scene—that is, put it into a book, write about it, claim it and transform it for language. Like Holcomb for Capote, it is material, a journalistic bonanza. Wolfe looks out at Times Square and sees not an inexplicability to escape but a sublime and intense array of subjects ready—ripe—for putting into words. He sees texts.

And this, I would suggest, is precisely what we experience when we read Wolfe. In the act of reading we experience the ordering textures and rhythms, the playfulness and irony, the intense metaphorical images, of Wolfe's language. We do not look completely past the language to its object. We experience style. The social and rhetorical significance of Wolfe is located here, in the act of reading. What Wolfe accomplishes for us is a stylistic transforming and ordering of realities that drive other writers to metadiscourse, irrealism, silence. That act of style itself, far from being purely mimetic, is a powerful argument for language at a time when language is being threatened by violence, unmeaning, and indifference.

2/ Truman Capote

A Ceremony of Style

I

Much has been said in recent criticism about what makes the nonfiction novel novelistic, what makes nonfiction fictive, and in most of these discussions Capote's *In Cold Blood* is a prominent example. Its textures and subtle symbolisms give it the feel of a novel. But in all the debate about the epistemological status of subject matter and the truth or falsity of characterization in the nonfiction novel, no one has recognized that one of the key similarities between fiction and nonfiction in Capote is the use of authorial silence. Capote's nonfiction is like his fiction in what it does not say, and this is true not only in *In Cold Blood* but in all the other major nonfiction as well.

By "silence" I mean that throughout his narratives Capote remains silent about important details, avoiding explicit interpretation and commentary. He repeatedly puts himself in the position of an outside observer forced to make inferences and read meanings on the basis of external detail. Silence in this sense is the underlying metaphor throughout Booth's *Rhetoric of Fiction*. Unlike eighteenth and nineteenth century narrators who comment directly on their stories, the silent author of modern fiction, according to Booth, has "effaced himself, renounced the privilege of direct intervention." The modern narrator "leaves his characters to work out their own destinies and tell their own stories"—he gives "the illusion that he is sitting silently behind scenes" of the story itself (7, 273, 50).

Silence in this sense is also related to Wolfgang Iser's notion that the reading experience depends on "gaps" or "blanks," the gaps arising from dialogue, for example, or from unexplained events, delayed revelations, and uninterpreted concrete images. At these junctures, "what *is* said only appears to take on significance as a reference to what is not said; it is the implications and not the statements themselves that give shape and weight to the meaning" (168). In the space left by the withdrawal of the narrator, meaning takes place. Information withheld, intepretation withdrawn, the reader is left to draw inferences and make connections.

In *Other Voices, Other Rooms*, for example, Capote's first and perhaps most representative novel, the narrator is silent for most of the story about Joel's father. Joel has come to Skully's Landing to live with a father he has never known, but from the beginning of his stay no one will tell him anything about the man—where he is, what he is like, when he can see him:

> "Miss Amy," he said, as they started down the stairs, "where is my dad? I mean, couldn't I see him, please, ma'am?"
> She did not answer. (50)

As narrator Capote doesn't answer this question either. He deliberately withholds information and interpretation throughout the first half of the novel. We know no more than Joel. With him we must explore the strange, silent house and deal with its enigmatic inhabitants—Randolph, Miss Amy—drawing what conclusions we can. At one point Joel hears a strange thumping on the stairs. It stops, there is "an instant of quiet," "then an ordinary red tennis ball roll[s] silently through the archway" (87). Later we find that this is a signal from Joel's invalid father for Randolph or Amy to come upstairs, but at this point it is a strange, mysterious sign, silent and uninterpreted. Like many other events and details in the novel, it puzzles Joel and it puzzles us. Capote leaves us with Joel to work out its significance.

Just as importantly, silence has to do with the way Capote

dramatizes rather than explicates his central themes, relying on symbolism and the implications of concreteness to convey meaning. He shows rather than tells. In the conclusion of *Other Voices* Joel stands in the garden at Skully's Landing and looks up at the clouds: "The clouds traveled slower than a clock's hands, and, as he waited, became thunder-dark, became John Brown and horrid boys in panama hats and the Cloud Hotel and Isabel's old hound, and when they were gone, Mr. Sansom was the sun." There is a sense of anticipation now. Something, some revelation, is about to take place:

> His mind was absolutely clear. He was like a camera waiting for its subject to enter focus. The wall yellowed in the meticulous setting of the October sun, and the windows were rippling mirrors of cold, seasonal color. Beyond one, someone was watching him. All of him was dumb except his eyes. They knew. And it was Randolph's window. Gradually the blinding sunset drained from the glass, darkened, and it was as if snow were falling there, flakes shaping snow-eyes, hair: a face trembled like a white beautiful moth, smiled. She beckoned to him, shining and silver, and he knew he must go: unhurried, not hesitating, he paused only at the garden's edge where, as though he'd forgotten something, he stopped and looked back at the bloomless, descending blue, at the boy he had left behind. (230–31)

Many threads of symbolism and implication developed from the beginning of the novel come together here, too complicated to explicate now. For our purposes it is enough to note that Capote does not explicitly comment on Joel's rite of passage. The moment is fundamentally symbolic, rendered concretely rather than openly interpreted. We must *read* the detail. On one level Joel is leaving the garden of his youthful innocence. On another he has learned the importance of passively accepting the darkness around him as the only way of escaping that darkness. He has come to see his father, Mr. Sansom, free of the clouds that have always surrounded him. He has come to accept Randolph, his sexually ambiguous cousin, who apparently is the mysterious woman he has repeatedly glimpsed in the upstairs window. In the moment in the garden, a moment where nothing essentially "happens" in any external sense—where everything, in fact, is literally silent—Joel moves from boyhood to manhood, although in Capote's rich silence it is unclear how full or healthy this manhood will be.

As in all literary expression, it is the concrete details of the dramatized situation that carry the weight of meaning. Capote does not "say" what he means here. What he says is the scene itself; what he means is what the scene implies, points to, causes us to think about for ourselves. This is the strategy in all of Capote's fiction, from the early stories to the later novels. He grounds his narratives in uninterpreted concrete images and leaves his characters ambiguous and enigmatic. It's not that we don't have any sense of the symbolic value of these images or characters. Capote provides us with clues throughout the stories to their philosophical and psychological importance, establishing their meaning through pattern and implication. The point is that as narrator Capote does not establish these correspondences directly. He is Booth's modern narrator, sitting silently behind the scenes as his characters deal with mysterious and troubling circumstance. He is Weaver's new rhetorician, relying on pictorial realism and photographic detail to convey meaning rather than engaging in panoramic commentary.

In this large sense, Wolfe, too, employs authorial silence, for the most part remaining detached from his narratives, allowing his characters to work out their own fates and speak for themselves, implying rather than stating his own interpretation of events. Though we would not associate Wolfe, in his intensity and verbosity, with silence in any narrow meaning of the word, he is remarkably similar to Capote in his decision to remain behind the scenes or within character.

The rhetorical effect of these silences is twofold. First, they draw us as readers into the action. In the absence of explicit commentary, we are made to "assemble" the text ourselves, generate meaning from the "instructions" implicit in the narrative. As Iser puts it, "the unwritten aspects of apparently trivial scenes and the unspoken dialogue within the twists and turns not only draw the reader into the action but also lead him to shade in the many outlines suggested by a given situation, so that they take on a reality of their own" (168). Gaps are the places of reconstitution in the act of reading, creating moments of what Iser would call "indeterminacy" in which we must discover or anticipate the meaning ourselves.

Second, and perhaps somewhat at odds with the first, silences demand reading. A silence does not readily disclose its meaning. It exists by definition in the absence of speech, in the absence, therefore, of explicit explanation. It requires interpretation. Although silences present us with puzzles which we are drawn toward assembling—although they invite us, or entice us, to fill in the gaps—they also require us to work harder as readers. The narrator is not doing all the work for us. We must participate. We must see past the words on the page, make connections between the dramatization before us and the larger themes it implies.

In fact, Iser differentiates between fiction and nonfiction, or what he calls "expository" prose, in precisely these terms. In a fictional text "connectability" is broken up by blanks and meaning becomes "multifarious." But in an expository text, he says, a text which "unfolds an argument or conveys information," the goal is to narrow down the "multiplicity of possible meanings" "by observing the connectability of textual segments." That is, exposition depends on explicitness. The expositor is to make his connections as clear as possible, his conclusions obvious and readily understandable. The reader should not have to fill any gaps or participate in the work of meaning. The utterance should be continuously "individualized," the meaning made as "precise" as possible (184).

In this light it is all the more interesting that Capote's nonfiction, like his fiction, depends on the rhetoric of silence. At the end of "A Duke in His Domain," Capote sums up his impressions of Brando, not with explicit commentary and interpretation, a direct analysis of character, but with a description of Brando's image—"sixty feet tall," his head "as huge as the greatest Buddha's"—projected on a billboard above a Tokyo theatre. It is an ironic portrait, and the irony depends on understatement: "Rather Buddha-like, too, was his pose, for he was depicted in a squatting position, a serene smile on a face that glistened in the rain and the light of a street lamp. A deity, yes; but, more than that, really, just a young man sitting on a pile of candy" (*Dogs Bark* 353). The last sentence here, the last sentence of the piece, is the only place where Capote does more than record, select, synthesize his impression of surfaces, and this is spare, restrained. The piece resolves itself in an image, a concrete detail from Capote's actual experience with obvious symbolic implications. In an earlier essay, "A Ride through Spain," Capote concludes a description of the Spanish landscape with a similarly evocative image, a one sentence paragraph that emphasizes the blank space at the end of the page: "The train moved away so slowly butterflies blew in and out of the windows" (*Dogs Bark* 104). There are no apostrophes here to the beauty of Europe or the end of an era. There is just the recreation of the scene itself, concrete and compact.

Capote claims a degree of omniscience in *In Cold Blood*, entering the minds of his characters and occasionally describing their feelings and attitudes—feelings and attitudes he has carefully reconstructed from extensive interviews. But it is significant that for the most part he renounces omniscience and maintains authorial silence in the narrative, withdrawing to the point of view of an outside observer restricted to making deductions from available evidence and testimony.

In the beginning Capote is careful to foreshadow the impending murder. Mr. Clutter heads for home and the day's work, "unaware that it would be his last"; Nancy lays out her prettiest red dress, "the dress in which she was to be buried" (13, 56). As narrator, these phrases suggest, Capote is in possession of the facts but is withholding what he knows as he prepares for the climax. When the climax finally comes and Dick and Perry drive their car up the Clutter driveway, Capote immediately cuts away, turning to a description of how the bodies were discovered rather than detailing the events of the murder itself. In fact, it is not until Perry's confession in the last half of the book that we know what exactly happened that night. Between this first section of preliminaries, "The Last To See Them Alive," and the third, "The Answer," he inserts a second, "Persons Unknown," establishing the character of Dick and Perry and detailing the reaction of the townspeople to the murder. Throughout this long intervening section he remains silent about the central event of the narrative.

As a result, we must join Alvin Dewey, the detective in charge of the case, as he struggles to decipher clues. With him we must try to account for the position of the bodies, the nature of the wounds, the state of the house. In the absence of answers, we must form hypotheses. It's "like those puzzles," Dewey himself puts it, "the ones that ask, 'How many animals can you find in this picture?'" (83). The animals are hidden for us precisely because of Capote's authorial silence. He doesn't tell us what he knows.

Capote continually puts us in the position of reading externals, even in the most apparently trivial scenes. Mrs. Clutter's room is austere, without personal ornament, "as though by keeping this room impersonal, by not importing her intimate belongings but leaving them mingled with those of her husband, she lessened the offense of not sharing his quarters" (29). The handwriting in Nancy's diary varies from entry to entry, sometimes slanted to the right, sometimes to the left, sometimes round, sometimes steep, "as though she were asking, 'Is this Nancy? Or that? Or that? Which is me?'" (57). "As though" conjectures are a necessary response to silence. Without the certainty of fact we can only deduce internals from the character of externals. Even near the end, when Perry is captured and brought in for questioning, Capote chooses to present him to us from a distance. With the detectives we view him through the one-way observation window of the interrogation room, deducing what we can from his "stiff Indian hair," his "pert, impish features," his flickering, lizard-like tongue (224).

It is from this perspective that we can understand the symbolic resonances characteristic of *In Cold Blood*. The cats who fish through the gutters for dead birds outside the courthouse are meant to be symbolic of people within the story—Dick and Perry, the journalists coming to cover the murder (258). Capote notes that over a Las Vegas motel where the police are searching for the killers the "R" and the "S" are missing from "rooms." The truncated word "OOM" seems to resonate in the rest of the story, a symbol of the disintegration of language and meaning in the face of violence (174). Earlier in this section Capote records part of a radio broadcast that awakens a prisoner in the Kansas State Penitentiary ("Chancellor Konrad Adenauer arrived in London today for talks with Prime Minister Harold Macmillan. . . . President Eisenhower put in seventy minutes going over space problems and the budget for space exploration with Dr. T. Keith Glennan" [159]), subtly linking the events that took place in Holcomb, Kansas, with world events on the eve of a new decade. These details are all presumably "true," yet selected from their context they assume a symbolic, evocative value beyond their literal meaning. As in Capote's fiction, concreteness does not mean what it says; it points beyond itself, evokes via association or metaphor something not stated.

In his later nonfiction Capote continues to assume an objective point of view, only this time eschewing omniscience entirely and acknowledging the perceiving "I." In "Hello Stranger" (*Chameleons*), he presents without commentary a conversation with a friend who confesses a strange sexual indiscretion. The sketch is constructed around the interview form itself—"TC's" question followed by "George's" answer—with a minimum of connecting description. The surface of the story and of the man who tells it are presented, without explicit interpretation, for us to judge. In "Handcarved Coffins" (*Chameleons*), a longer nonfiction piece reminiscent of *In Cold Blood*, Capote again features the bare skeleton of the interview, the give-and-take of question and answer without the narrator's all-seeing interventions. Occasionally he adds, in tight, almost minimalist parentheses, some description of the surrounding scene or landscape. There is never commentary. Here in these later pieces there are just the lineaments of the act of experiencing itself, the "I" in its immediate transactions with the world. By making himself nominally present in the story, Capote emphasizes silence even more than in *In Cold Blood*. Acknowledging the "I" in its act of observation calls our attention to the opaqueness of surfaces we must interpret for ourselves.

In an important statement in a *Paris Review* interview, Capote identifies this kind of rhetorical silence as the common strategy of both his fiction and his nonfiction:

> In reporting one is occupied with literalness and surfaces, with implication without comment—one can't achieve immediate depths the way one may in fiction. However, one of the reasons I've wanted to do

reportage was to prove that I could apply my style to the realities of journalism. But I believe my fictional method is equally detached—emotionality makes me lose writing control: I have to exhaust the emotion before I feel clinical enough to analyze and project it, and as far as I'm concerned that's one of the laws of achieving true technique. (Cowley 291)

In a sense the rhetoric of silence is more appropriate to nonfiction than to fiction. After all, in nonfiction the author cannot finally claim total omniscience. Capote can't say with absolute certainty why Nancy Clutter varies her handwriting, because she is a real person, not a fictional creation of his own. He can't say why Mrs. Clutter would keep her separate bedroom so austere, because he cannot read her mind. The rhetoric of silence acknowledges the limits of factual reporting. But at the same time Capote recognizes that the rhetoric of silence is the central strategy of his fiction (and, we would add, of most modern fiction). The technique of reading "surfaces" and making inferences from those surfaces is a choice for the novelist in a way it cannot be for the nonfiction writer, but its purposes and effects are the same in both modes. There is still the same insistence on the reader participating in the making of deductions, still the narrator's refusal to speak in his own voice and comment on the meaning of the action he has dramatized, the character he has described. The key to technique in both modes is "detachment"—control, distance, concreteness, the dramatization rather than explication of events. Both fiction and nonfiction depend, in this view, on "implication without comment."

Thus Capote's nonfiction has the same two contradictory rhetorical effects as his fiction. It elicits and at the same time demands a reading. It draws us into the narrative and at the same time makes it harder for us to understand the meaning of the words before us. Unlike more conventional narrative exposition, where everything is spelled out as completely as possible in its turn, Capote's nonfiction develops from implicitness, restraint, withholding. It is riddled with at least temporary moments of indeterminacy.

In a series of prefaces to his various collections of nonfiction, Capote has discussed his effort over a career to fashion a prose style of understatement and conciseness. He has striven, he says, for a "technical virtuosity as strong and flexible as a fisherman's net," a sentence structure "simple, clear as a country creek" (*Chameleons* xviii). This involves cutting and condensing, a radical revising away of what he perceives as the former "density" of his prose so that he can achieve the same effects in a single paragraph that he achieved before in three pages (vii). Or as he puts it in the preface to *The Dogs Bark*, he is struggling to control his "static" writing, "to reveal character and sustain mood unaided by a narrative line" (xviii), an interesting parallel to Wolfe's stated intention of developing narrative through "scene-by-scene reconstruction" with as little "historical narration" as possible. In the terms I have been developing, it seems clear that what Capote is really describing here is the rhetoric of silence, an attempt to create language which means more than it says, which shows rather than tells, which depends in the end on the author's strategic decision to stay out of what is ultimately pure narration and description.

Capote says it best, perhaps, in a tribute to the style of Japanese art. In his view all Japanese art depends on the "dread of the explicit." Thus, "the single blade of grass describing a whole universe of summer, the slightly lowered eyes left to suggest the deepest passion." The withholding of interpretation, the restraining of comment, is "all a ceremony of Style, a phenomenon that seems to rotate, in a manner quite separate from emotional content, on absolute style alone" (*Dogs Bark* 356). This is a spare and understated piece in itself, no more than 500 words long, richer in implication than in analysis. It is a fitting critical analysis of the rhetoric of silence, even though the word "silence" is never mentioned. In Capote, too, a blade of grass is "left" to describe the whole universe of summer, lowered eyes left to suggest deeper realities of character.

II

There is another dimension of silence in Capote, not just technical but thematic. Capote's fiction and nonfiction are saturated with explicit references to silence—the silence of landscape, of character, of scene and event. In *In Cold Blood* in particular silence becomes the central figure for the inexplicability of contemporary

American experience: it defines Capote's effort to communicate experiences which are fundamentally nonverbal or antiverbal.

Mr. Clutter is a speech-maker, a man used to standing up and talking to hundreds of people at the Rotary or the 4-H. He can "convince anybody about whatever," according to a friend (36). "No matter what the situation was, he could talk his way out of it" (117). Language is community. It provides the structures and continuities and contacts that govern everyday experience.

But as Perry explains in his confession, language fails on the night of the murders. Mr. Clutter can't convince Dick and Perry that he doesn't have a safe, then can't talk them out of the violence to follow. "You couldn't argue with him," Perry says of Dick, "he was so excited" (239). When Mr. Clutter tries to calm Dick down, Dick shouts: "Shut up! When we want you to talk, we'll tell you" (238). Violence takes place after the failure of language. It is fundamentally nonverbal, a rejection of the compromises and accommodations that language can make possible.

The act of murder is oddly noiseless in Perry's account. "The only sound was the wind," he remembers (236). Despite the noise of the shotgun blasts, no one hears anything unusual. As Capote subtly emphasizes, violence is a silencing: the plan of the murder, he says, was flawlessly devised, "from first footfall to final silence" (37). When Nancy's friend Susan comes to pick her up for church the next morning, she is struck by the similarly unnatural quiet of the aftermath. "Everything looked too bright and quiet," she says in a later statement (59). The other friends who discover the bodies also experience that unnerving soundlessness. The normal chatter and flow of phatic conversation has ceased in this family.

As the investigation into the murders proceeds, the silence of the Clutter house comes to figure the inexplicability of the event. In an essay on the filming of the movie *In Cold Blood*, Capote remarks that it is "a curious experience to find myself once more in this house where I have so often been, and heretofore under such silent circumstances: the silent house, the plain rooms, the hardwood floors that echo every footstep, the windows that look out on solemn prairies and fields tawny with wheat stubble"

(*Dogs Bark* 398). In *In Cold Blood* itself he uses similar imagery to describe Dewey's perceptions of the house:

> The detective moved from room to room. He had toured the house many times; indeed, he went out there almost every day, and, in one sense, could be said to find these visits pleasurable, for the place, unlike his own home, or the sheriff's office, with its hullabaloo, was peaceful. The telephones, their wires still severed, were silent. The great quiet of the prairies surrounded him. He could sit in Herb's parlor rocking chair, and rock and think. (152–53)

Later, too, Capote describes Nancy's boyfriend returning to the house, only to find it "shadowed, and hushed, and motionless" (207).

Despite the apparent peacefulness of these scenes, the silence surrounding the murder is maddening for Dewey and the other detectives involved in the case, maddening as well for the townspeople. The facts of the case, and the reasons for them, will not declare themselves. They constitute a kind of text to be read. "Writing has this strange quality," Socrates explains to Phaedrus, a quality it shares with painting. If one asks the creatures in a painting any questions, "they preserve a solemn silence." If one questions written words in the hope of better understanding their meaning, "they always say only one and the same thing" (69). So, too, with the silent texts in *In Cold Blood*. They simply reiterate themselves rather than refining, extending, explicating their mysteries: Why wasn't Nancy bound and gagged like the rest of the family? Were there two murderers? Is it just coincidence that Mr. Clutter took out a forty-thousand dollar life insurance policy the day of the murder? More importantly, why were the murders committed? Revenge? Robbery? For Dewey the silent details of the house—the physical evidence left at the scene, silently declaring itself over and over—don't "add up." "It doesn't make sense. But then, come right down to it, nothing does" (83).

Even though the details of the case are eventually resolved, over the course of the narrative the murder assumes a symbolic importance greater than its superficial mysteries of fact. Ultimately it is linked to a pervading sense of meaninglessness in the community and the nation as a whole. After all, Garden City is "just another fair-sized town in the middle—almost the exact middle—of the continental United States" (33). It is central, representative of the heartland. And the Clutters are representative of the city. A resident says of them, "I never heard a word against them; they were about as popular as a family can be, and if something like this could happen to *them*, then who's safe, I ask you?" (70). When the Clutters are murdered the community is threatened; their pain and horror are not just personal but an enactment of universal horrors. The Clutter murder is just one of many multiple murders beginning to take place throughout the country (271). The order of society seems to be threatened by bursts of arbitrary violence symptomatic of some intrinsic unrest or instability in the structure of things. It is the eve of a new decade. In the background are radios announcing the progress of the space program and new attempts to accommodate the Russians. The Bible admonition on Mrs. Clutter's bookmark evokes the mood of the times: "Take ye heed, watch and pray: for ye know not when the time is" (30).

In perhaps the most telling statement of all, a schoolteacher links the Clutter murders with a kind of existential dread:

> Feeling wouldn't run half so high if this had happened to anyone *except* the Clutters. Anyone *less* admired. Prosperous. Secure. But that family represented everything people hereabouts really value and respect, and that such a thing could happen to them—well, it's like being told there is no God. It makes life seem pointless. I don't think people are so much frightened as they are deeply depressed (88)

If God exists and is just, how could the Clutters be murdered? If God can be silent when people are suffering, can he be just? Can he exist? The murders in Holcomb raise the possibility that the world is not governed by a benevolent deity. Because they are apparently random and senseless—because no reason for them is discernible—they threaten to undermine the faith and values of the community. In this sense they come to represent the general malaise of the decade to come. The murder of the Clutters becomes for Capote a representative anecdote for dramatizing the fearfulness and uncertainty of contemporary American society.

In the face of such mystery and meaninglessness, language repeatedly fails. Ironically, the silent text of the event in *In Cold Blood* generates many other texts. Wordlessness engenders pages of ultimately futile testimony and interpretation. The detectives, of course, generate their "theories" and "hypotheses": that there were two murderers, that the motive was robbery, that the murderers were not known to the Clutter family, and so on—hypotheses which are then written up and recorded in volumes of police reports. Dewey goes on to formulate theories about the character of the murderers to account for some of the anomalies at the scene, for example, the fact that Bonnie and Nancy were tied up and then tucked into bed before they were shot or that a pillow was put under Kenyon's head. "At first I thought maybe the pillow was put there to make his head a simpler target." But "now I think, No, it was done . . . to make the victim more comfortable." One of the murderers at least exhibits a certain "twisted tenderness" (103). The townspeople also try to interpret and understand. Was it someone from town or one of the surrounding farms? Had Mr. Clutter made enemies? Was it Nancy's boyfriend? And there are conjectures about the motives. All are duly recorded—Mother Truitt's, Mrs. Clare's, the schoolteacher's, the friends'. Similarly, the newspapers write their blurbs and headlines trying to account for the murders: "a tragedy, unbelievable and shocking beyond words" (69). Eventually, convinced that the case will never be solved, the newsmen leave Garden City (113).

Perry's father and sister both write long letters which try to account for Perry's personality and motives. His father's manuscript, entitled "A History of My Boy's Life," details Perry's birth, childhood, education, jobs, even "recreation" and "interests." He was a "normal" boy, Mr. Perry insists, raised with the golden rule, sensitive and artistic. There are possible explanations here for Perry's behavior, hints that Capote later develops himself: an accident that left Perry crippled, perhaps damaged his brain; more importantly, and this Mr. Perry suggests only inadvertently, fatherly neglect and abuse. Yet as text the letter says more about the father than the son. Mr. Perry cannot express himself well enough to persuade us that his son should be paroled—the purpose of the letter—or give us insight into the murders he later commits (125–30).

Perry's sister, Barbara, also writes to persuade, this time to persuade her brother to reform his ways. The letter is full of attempts to explain why he has turned out the way he has. "I truthfully feel none of us have *anyone* to blame for *whatever* we have done with our own personal lives," she says, yet "of course, environment plays an awfully important part in our lives"—an allusion to the influence of their father. More important than the content of the letter, however, is the fact that it is another text which tries to interpret and which must in turn be interpreted. In fact, a prison counselor and confidant responds to the letter with a intricately reasoned piece of rhetorical criticism. "It is a foolish letter, but born of human failing," Willie-Jay writes. It fails in its objectives. "What could be *more* conventional than a housewife with three children, who is 'dedicated' to her family???? What could be more natural than that she would resent an unconventional person." Her letter "failed because she couldn't conceive of the profundity of your problem—she couldn't fathom the pressures brought to bear upon you because of environment, intellectual frustration and a growing tendency toward isolationism" (143–145). Willie-Jay is right in his analysis that ultimately communication is impossible between two people from two such different worlds. In the end language can only beget more language, text lead to text.

Perry himself provides texts in the form of notebooks, lyrics, and poems piled up in two heavy boxes, although there doesn't seem to be any order in the language. The notebooks consist of a nonalphabetical dictionary of useful words and an anthology consisting of obscure facts, poems, and literary quotations. He quotes from a Blackfoot Indian chief, "What is life? It is the flash of a firefly in the night. It is a breath of a buffalo in the wintertime" (147). His confession is also a text, recorded and then transcribed on paper. It is his own effort to explain in language the silence of his act. "It was like I was outside myself," he tells the detectives.

"Watching myself in some nutty movie." Mr. Clutter strikes him as a gentleman, "soft-spoken." "I thought so right up to the moment I cut his throat." Later: "I aimed the gun. The room just exploded. Went blue. Just blazed up. Jesus, I'll never understand why they didn't hear the noise twenty miles around" (240–44).

Still more texts develop in the trial. There is the academic language of the forensic psychiatrist, later published in an article in *The American Journal of Psychiatry*: Dick and Perry are "predisposed to severe lapses in ego-control which make possible the open expression of primitive violence, born out of previous, and now unconscious, traumatic experiences" (299). There is the language of the prosecution, oratorical rather than clinical, ascribing motives in its own way: "These were strange, ferocious murders. Four of your fellow citizens were slaughtered like hogs in a pen. And for what reason? Not out of vengeance or hatred. But for money. *Money*" (304).

For that matter, Capote's omniscient narration itself is a matter of textuality, since it is based on extensive interviews and exhaustive review of all the available transcripts from the police and the trial. Everything Capote is able to say about Perry's inner state or Clutter's frame of mind is grounded in the language of others, first spoken and then transcribed. It is all documented, in the literal sense, based on documents.

But in the end, even after the details of the murder are sorted out, the mystery persists: "The confessions, though they answered questions of how and why, failed to satisfy his [Dewey's] sense of meaningful design. The crime was a psychological accident, virtually an impersonal act; the victims might as well have been killed by lightning. Except for one thing: they had experienced prolonged terror, they had suffered" (246). It is not just the reason for the murders that remains inexplicable. The imagination fails to comprehend the quality and degree of the suffering the Clutters endured. Even Perry himself cannot explain what happened. Despite all the psychological and forensic and journalistic jargon, the event is beyond language: "and yet—How can I explain this? It was like I wasn't part of it. More as though I was reading a story. And I had to know what was going to happen. The end" (240).

Perhaps Perry was driven by hatred of his father; perhaps he had lost his ability to reason and feel because of brain damage suffered in the earlier accident; perhaps he was victimized by society in some way. But in the end things just happened; at the key moment there is a blank: "I didn't realize what I'd done till I heard the sound. Like somebody drowning" (244). As Perry puts it in a prophetic statement early on, "The ineffable happens, things *do* take a turn" (37). The emphasis on textuality ironically heightens our sense of the original silence. All these texts are attempts through language to find meaning, yet all fail in the end.

Silences dominate all of Capote's work. He is obsessed with the implications of silence for character and mood, landscape and scene. The history of the household in *Other Voices* is too various and intricate for the child's mind of the narrator to understand. It is no accident that when Joel does finally meet his father, the old man is unable to speak more than a few monosyllables. It is no accident either that Capote describes the interiors and the landscapes of the novel as silent (27, 151, 187, 198, 216, 217). In "Miriam" a young girl suddenly appears in the life of an older widow, ghostlike, haunting. She doesn't explain herself, doesn't answer Mrs. Miller's questions. She is a silent apparition, appearing and disappearing without a trace. In the end, standing in her bedroom "in the hushed snow-city," Mrs. Miller "strives to shape a sentence" to save herself but fails, falling silent (*Tree of Night* 123). What's striking about the old man sitting across from Kay in "A Tree of Night" is his absolute silence. He is deaf and dumb, sitting with "mute detachment," unmoving, unresponsive. There is about the man's face a "shocking, embalmed stillness," a "mysterious silence" which finally overpowers the protagonist in the story's ambiguous conclusion (*Tree of Night* 203–04).

Brando is Buddha-like in "The Duke in His Domain," his answers contradictory and jumbled, significant silences punctuating his digressions and mumblings. Bob Quinn is enigmatic and self-contradictory in "Handcarved Coffins," a sophisticated and intelligent murderer who never betrays himself. There are unsolved mysteries in the nonfiction landscapes as well. New Orleans is a "secret place," a place of "silent, suffocated gardens" (*Dogs Bark*

22–23). Of Ischai Capote remembers the "silent, shadowless afternoons" when the "whispering people wander back and forth and through the piazza and into some secret dark" (*Dogs Bark* 86). He is compelled, he says in "Hidden Gardens," by the "concealed" and "secret delights" of certain cities like New Orleans, cities which will "always remain wrapped boxes, containers of riddles never to be solved" (*Chameleons* 193).

Indeed, there is a crucial sense in which silence is fundamental to the very enterprise of the New Journalism for Capote. *The Muses Are Heard*, Capote's first long work of nonfiction, describes the experiences of an American acting company traveling by train to Leningrad to perform *Porgy and Bess*. It is really a short parable about the impenetrability of appearances. For pages and pages Capote records every random detail in his immediate experience, much like the camera in cinéma vérité: snatches of scenery, little vignettes involving the actors and their entourage, glimpses of strangers, and, especially, bits of conversation. In the objective, documentary style characteristic of *The New Yorker*, where *Muses* was first published, every surface is duly recorded.

Near the end, in his only direct authorial comment on the experience, Capote attests to the impossibility of ever getting beyond mere surface, ever understanding the truth silently underneath the phenomena we sense every second in our daily lives. What really happened? Capote is asked about the actual performance of the opera: "There is no absolute truth in these matters, only opinion, and as I attempted to formulate my own, tried to decide what I was going to tell Shapiro, I stretched on the bed and switched out the light" (164). In acknowledging his own subjectivity, Capote puts the entire cataloguing of the previous pages in a new light. These random details take on significance precisely as random details: this is all we can know, he is saying, all that we can determine with any certainty—what we actually experience, not what these experiences might mean. There is no absolute truth. From this perspective the language problems of the travelers assume new importance as well. The difficulty of the Americans in trying to understand the Russians, and of the Russians trying to understand the Americans—particularly the subtly nuanced slang of the play itself—comes to figure the inability of all people finally to understand each other. We are locked inside ourselves; the interiors of others are finally inaccessible—silent.

In "A Day's Work," Capote follows a housekeeper through her daily routine, carefully observing details from the interiors she cleans—a "leather-framed photograph" of a "swarthy macho man," for example, a copy of *True Detective* magazine, lipstick on the sheets—all clues to the identity of the man who lives in the apartment. Capote's technique is to read character as it is manifested in physical things. But all the evidence in the apartments is evidence of isolation and despair, from girly magazines left out in a bachelor's studio to a plastic dildo in the bathroom of a single woman. The tenants live alone, unable to communicate with each other, their letters unanswered, their notes indecipherable. Neither Capote nor Mary, the housekeeper, can hope to understand or reach them. The inhabitants are literally and figuratively absent. The meaning behind their surfaces remains a thing-in-itself, unknowable. In the telling epitaph to *Other Voices*, quoted from Jeremiah, "the heart is deceitful above all things, and desperately wicked. Who can know it?" In the end of "A Day's Work" Capote tells Mary, "I'm praying for you," and she replies: "Don't pray for me. I'm already saved. (She takes my hand and holds it). Pray for your mother. Pray for all those souls lost out there in the dark" (*Chameleons* 166).

The mysteriousness of everyday existence is implicit in the controversy surrounding Capote's omniscience in *In Cold Blood*. How can he know that Dick swerved to hit a dog on the way back from the murders? How can he know Perry's dreams, or what Mr. Clutter was thinking as he stood on the morning of the murder and faced the house? These questions suggest our instinctive sense of the mysteriousness of character. Our conclusions about motives and feelings in the real world are always in the nature of conjecture. Critics have attacked Capote because he misrepresented the basketball skill of Nancy's boyfriend or got the facts wrong on the sale of Nancy's horse. Even fact is finally beyond certainty when the author is not inventing the story. Experience is too various and complex, too fine, to be represented completely in words.

In the acknowledgments to *In Cold Blood* Capote concedes this problem, carefully bracketing all of his subsequent omniscient observations. "All the material in this book not derived from my own observation," he says, "is either taken from official records or is the result of interviews with the persons directly concerned." Underneath the apparent omniscience is still a reliance on external indicators of internal states or second hand reports of past events. Capote must rely on written testimony which is by definition removed from the event itself, an interpretation of an individual. He cannot get at the truth. He can only make his interpretations on the basis of evidence. Perhaps this, in the end, is the attraction of nonfiction for Capote. He has given many accounts of why he moved from fiction to nonfiction at the turning point in his career, but perhaps after all it is his attraction to mystery which draws him to the nonfiction novel.

III

Authorial detachment can be a technique in any narrative, whatever the themes. It is not necessarily linked to the problems of wordlessness that concern us in this study. But the nuances and patterns of silence we have seen operating within Capote's texts give a new dimension to the silences *of* the text, establishing a thematic link between the narrative and the point of view of the narrative. The richness of silence as a theme in Capote creates an atmosphere, a set of symbolic resonances, in which narrative detachment and withholding become symbolically important in themselves.

When Capote focuses on the "great quiet of the prairies" which surrounds Dewey as he sits in Herb's rocking chair, and then falls silent himself; when he allows the chilling remarks of the townspeople to resonate without qualification or consolation or commentary ("if it can happen to them, who's safe I ask you?" or "well, it's like being told there is no God"); when he describes for a moment a hawk circling over the wheatfields, isolating the image, leaving it stark, enigmatic—whenever Capote records a significant detail or bit of conversation or glimpse of the landscape without comment in these climactic scenes, he forces us as readers to experience the wordlessness at the heart of the events in Holcomb. Because he remains silent as narrator, withholding interpretation, we find ourselves as readers in the same position as Dewey, the townspeople, Capote himself: we must read details, generate theories and hypotheses, speculate about meaning behind phenomena, all without knowing whether our speculations are valid.

When he refuses to arbitrate among the competing readings his characters offer, refuses to intrude as narrator to declare truth or even to offer a theory of his own, Capote traps *us* in language. For us, too, as for Dewey and the townspeople, the truth remains a thing-in-itself, unknowable. "I didn't realize what I'd done till I heard the sound"—Perry's statement is fundamentally opaque, meaningless. It reveals nothing. As language, as text, it only highlights a more fundamental silence. Capote's authorial detachment at this point—he does not comment on this statement, does not qualify it, interpret it in his own voice—forces us into the position of limited observers faced with the opaqueness of phenomena, statements.

When Capote does not tell us what the clues of the murder might mean, when he does not give us direct insight into the motives for the murders, when he does not betray his own presence in the situation, he is reinforcing on the level of the narrative frame the thematic implications of the story: "In the parlor, a sheet of music, 'Comin Thro' the Rye,' stood open on the piano rack. In the hall, a sweat-stained Stetson hat—Herb's—hung on a hat peg. Upstairs in Kenyon's room, on a shelf above his bed, the lenses of the dead boy's spectacles gleamed with reflected light" (152). The language is spare and constrained and resolutely superficial, restricted to what can be observed. Details are made present—the dead boy's spectacles—but nothing more. They are random, part of no pattern. Narrative detachment can heighten suspense and involvement in any context, but in the context of *In Cold Blood* the rhetorical effect is greater. Capote's authorial silence here enables us to experience the implication of *In Cold Blood* that the final meaning of the event is inexplicable: the sheet music and the glittering glasses are merely poignant details, not symbols or clues, reminders of the pointlessness and randomness of the murders. In what Capote doesn't say, we experience what can't be said. When we join Dewey in the struggle to interpret the evidence—accounting for the position of the bodies and the nature of the wounds—when we participate with him in discovering the "animals in the picture," we experience more than the narrative suspense of a murder mystery. Because point of view is implicated in the symbolic resonances of the text, all the dilemmas of language and expression in the story are played out in the very act of reading.

In the process, ironically, Capote succeeds in magnifying the presence of the wordless reality he cannot finally describe. Absence creates presence. It is a psychological fact that the dimly seen and far away appear larger and more imposing in the mind. Obscurity arouses curiosity and activates imagination. "As nothing that is wholly seen through has other than a trivial character," Thomas Carlyle says, "so anything professing to be great, and yet wholly to see through it, is already known to be false, and a failure" (17). Unmarred by partial and inadequate description, the unseen object of expression—what happened to the Clutters, why it happened, what it means—becomes interesting and compelling. As Perelman puts it, "one of the benefits resulting from the obscurity of certain texts" is that such obscurity "quickens the attention." The "very lack of precision" gives the object of expression "a mysterious, magical character" (145, 157). Kenneth Burke agrees that we must concede "the great persuasive power of mystery" (*Rhetoric of Motives* 278). In fact, this is the rhetorical principle at work in Iser's notion that gaps elicit participation. Because the rhetoric of gaps depends on the mystique of withholding, it is ideally suited for magnifying the presence of an experience that can't be reproduced in language.

Here, then, is the central problem of contemporary American nonfiction. Silences represent for Capote both the danger of apocalypse and the attraction of mystery, the disintegration of culture and the intensely personal revelations of the self. Wolfe defines the American experience as sublime and in some ways mystical, and he embraces that sublimity. In Capote there is a greater sense of impending catastrophe, of threat and fear—the violence at Holcomb represents the beginning of some dimly understood but powerful incursion of evil and anarchy. Yet there is also in Capote a greater preoccupation with the seductions and fascinations of secrecy and concealment. Capote is drawn to silence as he is drawn to the poetic, the imaginative, the nuanced and layered. Silence seems to represent for him the claims of a certain kind of transcendence.

The rhetoric of silence, furthermore, is Capote's response to this problem. Wolfe pushes the outside of the envelope of language through rhetorical intensification and figures of sublimity in an effort to reach an experience beyond the limits of conventional journalism. Narrative detachment, in a sense, is Capote's way of pushing the outside of the envelope in an effort to attain mystery, wordlessness. If explicit commentary is impossible, the writer must seek some indirect means of suggesting, pointing to, hinting at his subject. Silence is a means of indirection, of pointing. It gives the readers instructions for an operation of meaning they must perform themselves. It implicitly asks readers to assemble, infer, deduce for themselves what as text it cannot explicitly say. As rhetoric, it circumvents the problem of representation: it seeks to entice us to imagine what cannot be represented.

But Capote, unlike Wolfe, does not approach the problem of apocalypse head on. He does not make a direct assault. He does not strain and struggle like Wolfe in the effort at direct evocation. Rather, he adopts narrative detachment as a strategy from the beginning of the story, carefully positioning himself from the outset.

In the starkness and tension of Capote's spare sentences there is some sense of strain or failure. The absence of reconciling commentary in Capote can be regarded on a basic level as symptomatic of his inability to interpret the event, a kind of zero-degree interpretive stance. From this perspective we would say that Capote does not arbitrate among these competing readings of the central silence because as narrator the experience literally overwhelms him. He is not working for effect but, in the face of such extreme and shocking brutality, resigning all efforts to create effects. This is the implication of Zavarzadeh's general thesis in *The Mythopoeic Reality*. Capote eschews interpretation, Zavarzadeh would say, because the event he is trying to describe is "inherently ambiguous and so bizarre that it cannot be categorized as either factual or fictional by our current epistemological standards" (126). Or in Tony Tanner's more elegant phrasing, Capote gives the "illusion of art laying down its tools as helpless and irrelevant in front of the horrors and mysteries of life itself" ("Death in Kansas" 98).

The text itself gives cues for reading narrative detachment as a kind of shock. When the bodies are first discovered, Capote says, "nobody said anything"; they were "too stunned" (63). When the jurors are shown pictures of the bodies later at the trial, the courtroom grows "exceedingly silent" (281). "It just shut you up," a friend of Mr. Clutter remarks, "the strangeness of it" (78).

Even in the shorter pieces, in *Muses* or "A Day's Work," Capote's decision to remain outside events emphasizes in part the limits of language and the presence of something beyond it. More than acknowledging the boundaries of journalism, Capote's careful maintaining of objectivity and his refusal to advance more than minimal hypotheses implies on the level of the narrative itself that human understanding is inherently finite. "We live in the dark," he quotes from Henry James, "we do what we can, the rest is the madness of art" (*Chameleons* xv).

But even if this were true, as we have seen in Wolfe, the very breakdown of imagination can have the effect of signifying the grandeur and magnitude of the object in view. Zavarzadeh's notion that Capote is relinquishing all control in his narrative stance simply overlooks the figurative possibilities of failure. Yet in the end I don't think that the logic of the sublime operates in quite this way in Capote. Our impression as readers of Capote is that he is in complete control of his language in *In Cold Blood*, that he has adopted a certain strategy from the beginning and carefully maintained it throughout the text. As Capote explains in a preface, nonfiction presents him with a stylistic challenge, an opportunity to create new aesthetic effects and develop a tighter, more effective prose style:

For several years I had been increasingly drawn toward journalism as an art form in itself. I had two reasons. First, it didn't seem to me that anything truly innovative had occurred in prose writing, or in writing generally, since the 1920's; second, journalism as art was almost virgin terrain, for the simple reason that very few literary artists ever wrote narrative journalism. (*Chameleons* xiv)

This is not literature giving up on itself, the artist renouncing art before the chaos of the age. This is the statement of a craftsman exploring the possibilities of his medium. The rhetoric of silence is a device of language for creating certain effects. As Mailer puts it—in an important analysis we will return to later—Capote's style is a kind of "jewel," "superb" in its craftmanship and precision. Capote is one of those contemporary authors who in Mailer's view follows the prescription for style laid down by "the great physician Dr. James Joyce—'silence, exile, and cunning'" (*Cannibals* 99, 5).

"Cunning" is not exactly the right word to describe Capote; it underestimates the intensity of his commitment to language, implies a kind of insincerity. But at the same time it does express the quality of control and precision I have tried to identify in his prose, and with "silence" on the one hand and "exile" on the other it comes close to capturing the true character of his style. Indeed, the context of Mailer's discussion of Capote is a larger discussion of how contemporary American writers develop forms in direct response to the "apocalyptic" nature of the great "Beast" that is America. Capote's response to the wordless is "the ceremony of style," the strong and flexible "fishermen's net" of words. He comes to Holcomb equipped with a stylistic credo ideal for coping with the experience he eventually finds—which is perhaps no accident after all, since Capote's style in his previous works of fiction is intimately linked with a concern for human mysteries and silences. The style and subject in Capote call forth one another. This is not to diminish the tension between words and wordlessness in Capote, nor to exclude the rhetoric of the sublime from a consideration of his style. In Capote that negative logic is worked out in subtler ways. The relationship between words and wordlessness in his prose, because restrained, is tauter, more finely tuned. But the issue at stake for him is the same as for Wolfe and, we will see, for Mailer: the effort to communicate the incommunicable.

IV

In an interview after Capote's death, the Kansas lawyer who prosecuted Perry and Hickock questioned the moral and rhetorical purpose of *In Cold Blood*:

> I don't think there was one bit of redeeming social value in Capote's whole book. It was a successful idea that made him and a lot of other people a lot of money. It's a shame that our city has to be on the map for that thing. In the courthouse square, we have a statue of C. J. Buffalo Jones, our first mayor (in 1883). He should get the recognition. It's just unfortunate that we didn't have media hype back then. (Polman)

Behind the frustrated boosterism in this remark lie legitimate questions about the value and intended effect of *In Cold Blood*, questions shared by more sophisticated readers and critics.

Booth maintains that "in fiction the concept of writing well must include the successful ordering of your reader's view of a fictional world." The author "has an obligation to be as clear about his moral position as he possibly can be," whatever that moral position is (*Rhetoric* 388–89). In some modern fiction, where narrative detachment is too scrupulously maintained, the intelligent reader cannot be sure what the author is trying to imply. In his silence, we are subject to "misreadings."

If fiction has the obligation to interpret rather than simply present surfaces, nonfiction would seem to have an even greater obligation to order. Though fiction may have didactic purposes and specific rhetorical ends, its primary purpose is to create an aesthetically satisfying and credible fictive world. Rhetorical literature, in contrast, while it may have aesthetic and literary purposes, is by definition intended to serve rhetorical ends: it must inform, deliberate, reflect on experience.

It is possible to argue that Capote's stance in *In Cold Blood*, like Wolfe's in *Acid Test*, is morally ambiguous in precisely Booth's sense. Because he maintains a strict authorial silence in his nonfiction narratives, it is difficult to determine on a first or superficial reading whose side Capote is on or what he wants us to learn from the story. Because he does not argue or reflect in explicit ways, it is not immediately apparent how *In Cold Blood* is meant to inform us or guide us.

To put this another way, Capote can be seen as guilty of aestheticism. Weber rightly says of *In Cold Blood* that "no other work of literary nonfiction is so resolutely literary in its intentions" (74). As we have noted, Capote's own statements about the composition of the book are largely technical, his motives aesthetic. His sacrifices, he says, have been at "the altar of technique" (*Chameleons* xii). From this perspective the argument is that Capote is simply interested in creating aesthetic effects, not in responding to social problems. We know that Capote made the decision to experiment with nonfiction prior to discovering the subject of the Holcomb murders. The tragedy in Kansas seemed to be ideal material for creating a new, hybrid literary form.

At the same time it can be argued that in his silences Capote allows himself to identify—and allows us to identify—with Perry, just as Wolfe seems to allow us in his silences to identify with Kesey. In remaining strategically detached from the narrative, Capote engages our sympathy with a morally despicable criminal mind. In failing to correct or qualify the actions and thoughts of the mind he inhabits, Capote implicates himself in a kind of evil. More than that, it can be argued that Capote actively sympathizes with Perry's character and situation, identifying himself with Perry's appearance, his status as freak and victim, his artistic tendencies. In this light Perry becomes a prime example of what Booth calls the "seductive rogues who narrate much modern fiction." Inside views "can build sympathy even for the most vicious character," Booth points out, and while such strategies of identification can force us "to see the human worth of a character whose actions, objectively considered, we would deplore," they also run the risk of "moral confusion" (379).

But it seems to me that in my claims for the rhetorical effectiveness of silence in Capote are two important answers to these charges.

First, Capote's preoccupation in both his fiction and nonfiction is with demonstrating that the world contains silence and mystery. His underlying "moral" or "message" is that beyond the narrow and petty concerns of our day to day life are mysteries both terrible and compelling. Holcomb, like La Honda, is a metaphor for complacent Eisenhower Republicanism exploded by the energies of the age. Capote's quick sketch of the Clutters' living room suggests his subtle satire of the middle-class:

> As for the interior, there were spongy displays of liver-colored carpet intermittently abolishing the glare of varnished, resounding floors; an immense modernistic living-room couch covered in nubby fabric interwoven with glittery strands of silver metal; a breakfast alcove featuring a banquette upholstered in blue-and-white plastic. This sort of furnishing was what Mr. and Mrs. Clutter liked, as did the majority of their acquaintances, whose homes, by and large, were similarly furnished. (9)

The banal bad taste of this interior reflects the stolidity of the town as a whole. It is unimaginative. In an opening scene that recalls Wallace Stevens' "Disillusionment at 10 O'Clock" ("The houses are haunted / by white night gowns"), Capote describes Holcomb as a ghost-town, faded, empty, isolated. Its people are asleep, both literally and figuratively; they are "sufficiently unfearful of each other to seldom trouble to lock their doors" (5).

Into this landscape—figured by the silence of the deserted streets and the sleeping townspeople—come "explosions" and "foreign sounds" which foreshadow the murder. Until the murders, no "exceptional happening" had ever occurred in Holcomb. Capote's purpose from the beginning of the book, if read carefully, is to wake up the townspeople—and by implication, the reader. His silences are meant to stimulate our involvement and arouse us from complacency. They constitute both a warning and an invitation.

All the main characters in Capote's fiction are characters of imagination, enigmatic and beyond formula. As the Egyptian remarks in "A Jug of Silver," "It's the mystery that's enchanting" (*Tree of Night* 152). It's not the possibility of winning a great deal of money that inspires the townspeople to gamble on how many silver coins the druggist has stored up in a clear glass jug; the people are inspired by the sense of not knowing. A feeling of uncertainty and anticipation raises the characters in this story above their ordinary life. *The Grass Harp* is a parable about the power of Dolly's magic versus the deadening mechanicalness of her sister's insistence on formula. Dolly is a free spirit, close to the earth, a maker of magic potions, someone suspect from the standpoint of conventional standards of conduct. Verena, her sister, is authoritarian, no-nonsense, business-like, contemptuous of her sister's excesses and irresponsibility. At the crisis point, when after an argument Dolly runs away to live in a treehouse, Capote clearly means us to see, through the eyes of his young narrator, the desirability of the imaginative life over and against the life of convention. His sympathies, and ours, are with Dolly in the treehouse.

This is the whole tenor of Capote's work, from the early stories through the later nonfiction. He is compelled by mystery, and his argument, reinforced by the rhetoric of silence, is that mysteries have an intrinsic power and desirability. I'm not suggesting that in *In Cold Blood* Capote in some way prefers violence over peacefulness, murder over middle-class life. Yet there is in Capote's scrupulous avoidance of explanation, his insistence on the inexplicability of the event, a sense that for him there is value in some happening which challenges and raises us above the mundane inevitability of bourgeois life. "Things unspoken" are always "the center of interest," he remarks of Dick's interrogation (229).

If this is true, the rhetoric of silence, as style, performs its argument. Style is a kind of magic. It transcends simple communication, the transaction of information and fact. It exists as a kind of aura between the lines, in the blank space surrounding the text. Style develops from what is not said and what cannot be said. Perhaps from this perspective, what seems a mere "ceremony of style," a set of strategies open to the charge of aestheticism, really develops a philosophical and thematic force of its own. Style becomes an argument for style, for that which cannot be measured, explained, reduced to the explicit.

Indeed, in my view Capote's style is his most powerful argument. He is not morally ambiguous. He is not on Perry's side. He is on the side of language. The fact of his style, the fact even of his aestheticism, signals his allegiance to the controlling and conserving power of language over and against the chaos and violence and meaninglessness threatening language from the outside.

It is true that Capote identifies with Perry in certain very subtle ways. By means of the rhetoric of silence—selection, presence, connotation and imagery—he orchestrates our deepening engagement with Perry from the beginning of the book. After Perry is arrested and jailed Capote chooses to describe his situation through the eyes of Josie Meier, the sheriff's wife and Perry's cook during his imprisonment in Holcomb. Mrs. Meier is a kindly older woman, and her portrait of Perry emphasizes his vulnerability and even his gentleness: she worries about the large crowds that gather around the jail; she worries that Perry might catch pneumonia on the first "bitter cold" night; she frets because he doesn't eat any of his supper. Through her we later learn that Perry befriends a squirrel who appears on his window sill, that he cried on the night of his conviction, and that, after being sentenced to hang, he declared, "I'm embraced by shame" (308). He speaks softly, "almost a whisper," spends his time brooding quietly in his cell, standing at the window. Through Mrs. Meier's maternal eyes we see Perry as a lonely and suffering child in a thin cotton prison shirt. "He wasn't the worst young man I ever saw," she says (285). He becomes associated in her account with the homey pleasantries of apple pie and baked bread. The jail is adjacent to the Meiers' kitchen, the criminal subsumed for the moment in the domestic.

Capote has not made any explicit bids for our sympathy and compassion. He has remained detached. But just by his selection of Mrs. Meier's narrative as the organizing point of view at this juncture, and his suppression of other points of view, he has encouraged us as readers to identify with Perry. Throughout the book he selects detail and testimony that present Perry in a favorable light: Perry writes and paints, he is abused and abandoned by his father, he is deformed. According to Willie-Jay, a friend from prison, he is a frustrated poet, something "rare and savable" (45). The mere selection of such details, even without directing commentary, projects Perry's character in positive ways.

By withholding his description of the actual murders until late in the third section of the book, Capote further encourages us to sympathize with Perry. Unaware of the horrible and senseless details of Perry's behavior on the night of the killings, we are more likely to pity him for his tough luck and difficult childhood. When Capote does finally describe the murders themselves, he chooses to relay the details first through Perry's own confession. The killings are first presented through the consciousness of a character for whom we've developed some measure of sympathy. As Capote himself explained in an interview with George Plimpton:

> I believe Perry did what he did for the reasons he himself states—that his life was a constant accumulation of disillusionments and reverses and he suddenly found himself (in the Clutter house that night) in a psychological cul-de-sac. The Clutters were such a perfect set of symbols for every frustration in his life. As Perry himself said, "I didn't have anything against them, and they never did anything wrong to me—the way other people have all my life. Maybe they're just the ones who had to pay for it." Now in the particular section where Perry talks about the reason for the murders, I could have included other views. But Perry's happens to be the one I believe is the right one. (Plimpton 38)

What Capote describes here is what Perelman calls the rhetorical power of "choice" in creating "presence" (116). Because as readers we have only one interpretation to consider—because competing interpretations are set aside—we are more likely to give this version of events credence. It is more present in our minds, "overestimated" in our consciousness.

What Burke would call the "question-begging tonalities" of Capote's descriptive language also encourage identifications with Perry (*Rhetoric of Motives* 91). In the first pages of the book Capote describes Mr. Clutter with documentary style briskness. The sentences are direct and unadorned, the detail largely factual and statistical. We are told about his insurance policies, his membership in the Rotary, the value of his house and land. Clutter in fact comes off as something of a prig: "He did not smoke, and of course he did not drink; indeed, he had never tasted spirits, and was inclined to avoid people who had" (20).

But in the second chapter, simply spliced or juxtaposed after the first, the language becomes denser and richer, the character more imaginative and compelling. This is our first description of Perry:

> His own face enthralled him. Each angle of it induced a different impression. It was a changeling's face, and mirror-guided experiments had taught him how to ring the changes, how to look now ominous, now impish, now soulful; a tilt of the head, a twist of the lips, and the corrupt gypsy became the gentle romantic. His mother had been a full-blooded Cherokee; it was from her that he inherited his coloring—the iodine skin, the dark, moist eyes, the black hair which he kept brilliantined and was plentiful enough to provide him with sideburns and a slippery spray of bangs. (15–16)

Perry is not an entirely sympathetic character. He is vain, and as we learn later in the scene, he is also shiftless, out of work, and recently released from prison. But Capote's descriptions make him out to be a romantic, gypsy-like figure strikingly more interesting than the stick figure of Mr. Clutter. Perhaps more importantly, Capote's sentences become more heavily modified and sophisticated, not just base clauses followed by an appositive or two—the stock sentence of his prose—but long, accumulating descriptions, dense with metaphor, assonance, consonance, concrete detail ("the slippery spray of bangs," "the iodine skin"). Perry dreams of travelling to exotic places, of "drifting downward through strange waters, of plunging toward a green sea-dusk, sliding past the scaly, savage-eyed protectors of a ship's hulk that loomed ahead, a Spanish galleon—a drowned cargo of diamonds and pearls, heaping caskets of gold" (17). The poetic texture of the language both engages us and signals Capote's greater interest in Perry's character. Like Kesey for Wolfe, he is a figure of imagination, and the sentences that describe him are not transparent but translucent. The appositives lengthen and become more interesting, more metaphorical.

But ultimately Capote cannot be on Perry's side in this book because Perry represents the nonverbal and the antiverbal. It is clear that in some ways Capote saw himself in Perry; he shared with Perry the experience of deformity and isolation. It is also true that in *In Cold Blood* there are several indications that Capote views the hanging of the murderers as "pretty goddam cold-blooded, too" (306). But these are not the real issues. What Perry represents is the danger of the antiverbal and nonverbal forces which threaten American society on the eve of a new decade. He represents the rejection of language which precedes the act of violence, whatever his pretenses to poetry. Ultimately, after all the efforts to engage our sympathies, Capote reveals the facts of that night in Holcomb for what they are: a horrible silencing of the discourse that enables us to live together. Perry's silence is in some ways compelling: as a figure of imagination he embodies the possibility of transcending the mundane. But on a higher level he threatens to undermine the possibility of making sense out of the world through words.

It is from this perspective that Capote's style itself becomes the most important rhetorical act. The language presenting Perry's character and engaging our sympathies with him is at odds with the violence and wordlessness that Perry finally represents. The language that describes him controls, conserves, directs, maintains nuances and shades of meaning. Perry himself is not capable of writing the kinds of sentences that Capote uses to portray him or using the kinds of metaphor Capote discovers for suggesting his importance. His language is mumbled and fragmentary, incapable of managing his affairs in the world.

In Capote's silence and reticence we are called to read each word carefully, ponder its meaning. Capote's detachment requires us to linger on the surface of the language, drawing us into that contractual relationship that Iser describes as the filling of gaps. Ironically, the text invites our participation because it demands our interpretation. And as a result, in the experience of reading Capote, we are located in the text, we are inside it, recreating it ourselves, participating in the making of meaning. We are not implicated finally in Perry's evil but in Capote's aestheticism, his demand for and peformance of style. Because gaps create puzzles to solve, we are finally engaged with Dewey and the other detectives in the effort to establish order.

The priority of style over substance is what makes Capote's work socially valuable. It represents the battle of words against wordlessness. There is no real contradiction here. On the one hand Capote wants to create and celebrate silence, awakening his readers to experiences beyond words and in some way energizing language with the possibilities of silence. But on the other hand he wants to claim silence for language. He wants to identify with Perry's violence and mystery yet contain it for style. Silence for him does not represent the failure of rhetoric; rather, silence is the key to the dynamic possibilities of rhetoric.

3 / *[signature: Norman Mailer]*

The Record of a War

I

Ten years before Wolfe's *The Right Stuff*, Norman Mailer wrote *Of a Fire on the Moon*, in my view his most representative work of nonfiction. Mailer is concerned with Apollo 11, the first moon landing, while Wolfe's interest is Project Mercury, but the subjects of the books are fundamentally the same. Like Wolfe, Mailer is compelled by the energies and contradictions and metaphors embodied in the American space program. The books invite comparison. Because they have the same subject, they give us a particularly good opportunity to distinguish Mailer's style from Wolfe's, to see that Mailer's response to the problem of inexplicability is decidedly different from Wolfe's, or for that matter, from Capote's. In Mailer all the problems and issues we have been following are pitched higher. What in Wolfe and Capote are the subtle implications of form become in Mailer an active polemic. In Mailer, the tensions we have seen break out into a war.

Throughout his work Mailer is obsessed with the idea of sublimity and apocalypse. He needs to see his subject as beyond the threshold of the ordinary and everyday and to see himself in the act of challenging that limit. Even more than Wolfe and Capote, he habitually sees America as full of overpowering energies and contradictions. In *Of a Fire on the Moon* Mailer finds in the space program a particularly powerful and complex metaphor for this sense of the American experience:

> For it was true—astronauts had come to live with adventures in space so vast one thought of the infinities of a dream, yet their time on the ground was conventional, practical, technical, hardworking, and in the center of the suburban middle class. If they engaged the deepest primitive taboos, they all but parodied the conventional in public manner; they embarked on odysseys whose success or failure was so far from being entirely in their own control that they must be therefore fatalistic, yet the effort was enterprising beyond the limits of imagination. (46)

What the flight of Apollo 11 represents for Mailer is the dichotomy of America: on the one hand its sublimity, its inexplicability and greatness; on the other its mundaneness, its resistance to poetry and the expression of mystery.

On one level the flight of Apollo 11 is in a very specific sense sublime. It concerns "the infinities of a dream"; it is "enterprising beyond the limits of the imagination." Like the original Mercury astronauts in Wolfe's account of the space program, the Apollo astronauts are interesting to Mailer because they have experienced realities no one has experienced before. Their effort, particularly the first moon landing itself, strains credibility—the distances they must travel and the logistical problems they must master are beyond comprehension.

Mailer uses the technical vocabulary of sublimity to describe the mission from the beginning of *Fire*. He is overwhelmed, for example, by the Vehicle Assembly Building which houses the Apollo-Saturn vehicles. Its four tall bays are each thirty-six stories high, "high enough and wide enough to take in through their portals the UN Building or the Statue of Liberty." Its interior, an interlocking network of vast platforms and girders, is "a complexity of buildings within buildings which had been first maneuvered then suspended ten and twenty and thirty stories above the ground." It is an "unfinished and monumental cathedral," a "concatenation of structure upon structure, of breadths and vertigos and volumes of open space beneath the ceiling, tantalizing views of immense rockets hidden by their clusters of work platforms" (53–54). Later

Mailer dwells on other dimensions and statistics: the amount of fuel the rocket requires, the variety and extent of the wires and tubes and materials it contains, the millions of miles the astronauts will travel, the speed they will travel, the multitude of calculations that must be performed to guide their flight, the amount of money the mission will cost. This is what Kant called the "mathematical sublime" (86ff.). The mind is moved by the thought of numbers with dozens of zeros and by the impression of length and breadth without end. The effort to measure and the emphasis on calculation only suggest the immeasurable and incalculable. Only computers, only an abstract language of mathematical symbols, can encompass such immensity.

As Mailer puts it at the end of this scene:

> He was standing at least in the first cathedral of the age of technology, and he might as well recognize that the world would change, that the world *had* changed, even as he had thought to be pushing and shoving on it with *his* mighty ego. And it had changed in ways he did not recognize, had never anticipated, and could possibly not comprehend now. The change was mightier than he had counted on. The full brawn of the rocket came over him in this cavernous womb of an immensity, this giant cathedral of a machine designed to put together another machine which would voyage through space. Yes, this emergence of a ship to travel the ether was no event he could measure by any philosophy he had been able to put together in his brain. (55)

Might, brawn, immensity—in the face of this vastness and power, Mailer finds that "nothing fit anything any longer" (56).

There is more at stake here than the exceeding of measure. Mailer sees, too, in the flight of Apollo 11 experience "next to death itself" (111), an experience that puts us in touch with "that other world where death, metaphysics and the unanswerable questions of eternity must reside" (47). Involved are human courage, the willingness to risk great things for greater causes, the expression of longing for an Otherness, a beyond. He wants to see in the space program a poetry of the human spirit. In one of his recurring poses in *Fire* he regards the moon landing as the externalization of our desire to discover the origin of things, or to escape the ordinary. In this sense the space program is the realm of the "psychic outlaw," Mailer's Faustian culture hero seeking to experience the extremes of human nature. Space is the realm of an extreme, therefore, in both Wolfe's and Mailer's terms, of a heroism. It is the realm of power.

Mailer claims in the beginning of *Fire* that his "philosophical world" is built on the conviction that "nothing was finally knowable" (7). He is always looking, he says, for the secret behind the event. This is not just an existential position but an aesthetic credo. An idea or an event for Mailer is "beautiful because it [is] profound and it [is] mysterious" (45). Mailer is a writer looking for the big pay-off. Like Wolfe, he wants subjects where the stakes are high. He wants to measure himself against the grand. He wants material that contains the unknowable, and in the flight of Apollo 11 he finds such material. As subject, as event, it is "irreducible" (127)—it has no "objective correlative" (130).

Yet on another level the space program represents for Mailer not the extraverbal but the antiverbal. It figures for him the "cancer" that he has warned and fought against since *The Naked and the Dead* and "The White Negro." In a series of preflight news conferences the Apollo 11 astronauts—Armstrong, Aldrin, and Collins—reveal their inability to speak in any language but a technological "code" incapable of suggesting "philosophical meandering" or any nuances of feeling. Communication for them is merely "functional" (12–13). They refuse to reveal their feelings about the mission or to speculate about its larger implications. Their language is like "fortran," computer-generated, "impersonal, interlocking" (32). For them disasters become "contingencies"; the possiblity of "wandering through space, lost forever to life" is simply another variable under the category "trajectory conditions." Their formulations are "anti-dread," suppressing any "emotional symptoms" (25).

Wolfe, too, is concerned with the manly code of understatement and silence exemplifed by the test pilots. The right stuff is an "unspoken thing," both because it is privileged and beyond expression and because, even if it were within the province of language, it is a matter of personal feeling which real men keep to themselves. The code, Mailer agrees, is always to "keep your cool" (28).

In Mailer's philosophical system the "technologese" which the astronauts substitute for full expression is also linked with the same forces in society which result in shopping malls and fast food and the disappearance of the concrete, the individual, the nonstandard. It is symptomatic of what in *Cannibals and Christians* he calls the "plague" of American experience,

> that mysterious force which erects huge, ugly, and aesthetically emaciated buildings as the world ostensibly grows richer, and proliferates new diseases as medicine presumably grows wise, nonspecific diseases, families of viruses, with new names and no particular location. And products deteriorate in workmanship as corporations improve their advertising, wars shift from carnage and patriotism to carnage and surrealism, sex shifts from whiskey to drugs. And all the food is poisoned. And the waters of the sea we are told. And there is always the sound of some electric motor in the ear. (3)

Mailer's sympathies are very much in the romantic tradition: his causes are feeling and intuition versus the dominance of rational intellect, recalcitrant nature versus the dominance of technology, the energies of the individual self versus the standardizations of bourgeois social mores. Armstrong's extraordinary "remoteness" and Aldrin's one-dimensional preoccupation with trajectory mechanics are for Mailer representative of a trend in American society away from human value and toward the machine.

There is a sense of almost desperate prophecy in Mailer, and those prophecies are directed towards what he sees as the pending triumph of mechanism. "Apocalypse or debauch is upon us," he warns in *Cannibals and Christians*. "The sense of a long last night over civilization is back again" (2). His attitude in *Fire*, and throughout his work, is not unlike that of George Steiner in *Language and Silence*: language is being increasingly threatened by the incursion of mathematical and scientific symbologies which deny the validity of passion and value.

There is, too, in Mailer's antipathy towards the language of the astronauts an impatience with middle-class unimaginativeness. "The horror of the Twentieth Century," he says, is "the size of each new event, and the paucity of its reverberation" (34). Americans don't seem to know how to appreciate the sublimity of their own history. The "unequaled banality" of the astronauts' personalities is representative of the middle class failure to recognize the grand. All must be reduced to the practical, the utilitarian, and the hard-working. The astronauts, "the core of some magnetic human force called Americanism, patriotism, or Waspitude," appear in their news conferences more like junior corporate executives than epic heroes (315, 21).

The flight of Apollo 11, then, embodies "all the incomprehensible contradictions of America," contains in its "huge contradictions," "some of the profound and accelerating opposites of the century itself" (316, 47). Both extraverbal and antiverbal, it is symbolic of what Mailer calls our "most soul-destroying and apocalyptic" of times (47). Moreover, both poles of this dichotomy—and the dichotomy itself—generate a rhetorical dilemma for Mailer. Both the extraverbal and the antiverbal resist formulation. In agreeing to write an account of the flight to the moon, Mailer has involved himself in the recurring rhetorical challenge of American prose, the challenge of somehow communicating the incommunicable.

Mailer dramatizes his own situation as a rhetorical writer in his full description of the astronauts' first meeting with the press. They are, he says, technicians "debouched into the open intellectual void of the theatre" trying to communicate to the press, and through them to the general public. "Yaws abounded"—"vacuums." They do not know how to explain "the complexity of their technique." Armstrong "spoke with long pauses," searching for words, struggling to reduce his knowledge and experience to understandable phrases. These are "real" pauses, Mailer notes, "as if the next experience were ineffable but with patience could be captured" (21–22). Here as throughout his work, particularly in *The Armies of the Night*, Mailer is rhetorically self-conscious. He is constantly in the act of dramatizing and then analyzing the relationship between speaker and audience in real, concrete settings. And what he is suggesting in this analysis of Armstrong's language is the rhetorical impact of the dichotomy between the extraverbal and the antiverbal. Yaws abound and vacuums open up because Armstrong cannot work his way around the inexplicability of his object and his dedication to technologese. Mailer has respect for Armstrong as well as antipathy. His effort before the audience of the nation and the world is Mailer's own.

On both levels of the dichotomy, "events were developing a style and structure which made them almost impossible to write about" (88). "The century had unstrung any melody of words" (130). We have seen these claims for inexplicability before, but never more explicitly stated. The ineffable is the underlying problem in Wolfe and Capote, not, as here, the open and repeated thesis. And Mailer's mood and tone are more somber and threatened. Wolfe is confident and exuberant in the face of the sublimity of twentieth-century America. He wants to take it on. Capote carefully works out and then encourages an attraction to mystery and silence, even though, as we have seen, such silences carry an undertone of apocalypse and danger. But in Mailer we have moved completely from mystery to apocalypse. We don't want to mistake Mailer's own exuberance or his own willingness to embrace the sublime. The vacuums and breaches of American experience compel him as well. But even in his vitality and energy there is in Mailer a current of anxiety, a voice of warning and opposition. History, he fears, is moving in its contradictions and tensions towards some imminent catastrophe.

Mailer's stylistic response to this material is equally complex. There are in his prose some moments of direct evocation and rhetorical intensification very reminiscent of Wolfe. Mailer's description of the launch of Apollo 11, for example, is characterized by appositive intensification ("Then it came, like a crackling of wood twigs over the ridge, came with the sharp and furious bark of a million drops of oil crackling suddenly into combustion, a cacophony of barks louder and louder") and polysyndeton ("then came the earsplitting bark of a thousand machine guns at once, and Aquarius shook through his feet at the fury of this combat assault, and heard the thunderous murmur of Niagaras of flame roaring conceivably louder than the loudest thunders he had ever heard and the earth began to shake and would not stop"). He takes the event itself, statable in a single base clause, and then intensifies and expands it with additional description and detail. The event is contained in a single sentence which gathers momentum as it moves. Mailer's sentences are more solemn and measured than Wolfe's, the phrases of equal length, the diction more dignified and abstract. There are fewer interruptions. Whereas Wolfe's sentences depend on rhythmic intensifiers, Mailer's are more metaphorical ("like a ball of fire, like a new sun mounting the sky"). Yet at moments like these Mailer shares with Wolfe the strategy of rhetorical magnification. His rhythms and images reflect his excitement as he directly confronts the sublime experience (100–101).

But Mailer's characteristic response is not direct evocation at all. It is, rather, a metadiscursive self-dramatization antithetical to Wolfe. Unable to word the wordless, Mailer more often tells the story of his effort to word the wordless; unable to describe the event itself, he describes himself in the act of description. He is not silent, not invisible, not in the background.

There is a peculiar self-consciousness in the very phrasing of Mailer's prose. It sometimes appears deliberately awkward and artificial, as if calling attention to itself as language: "It occurred to him on the instant that one's fear of height . . ."; "Yes, one would have to create a psychology to comprehend the astronaut"; "For a beginning, however, it would be good to recognize . . ." (56). Each of these characteristic phrases is an example of metadiscourse. The language refers to itself and to the writer in the act of thinking through the problem in language. As Joseph Williams points out, words and phrases like "for example," "what I mean is," "in other words," and so on do not refer to a subject. Rather, they direct the flow of the words themselves by calling our attention to transition and intention. They signal that there is a writer behind the language with a point to make. And excessive metadiscourse in Williams' view is a source of wordiness and thus a problem to revise (47). For our purposes such phrases suggest Mailer's pervasive habit of self-reflexiveness and displacement. "We will be trying after all to comprehend the astronauts," he writes. "If we approach our subject via Aquarius . . ." (4). Or, "Well, let us make an approach to the astronauts" (18). At these and many other moments our attention as readers is skewed; we are made aware of the writer in the effort to compose.

Mailer calls attention to the process of composing more explicitly by recording the career of his moods. He feels "confirmation building in his mood, his happiness and his senses," as he begins to glimpse an underlying motive in the astronauts' psyche (48), but not long afterwards he finds that he is "bored" by the unrelenting mechanicalness of the flight itself. In fact, at this point he "could not forgive the astronauts their resolute avoidance of a heroic posture." (108). Yet soon, not more than a few hours later, he "discovered that he was happy. There was a man on the moon. There were two men on the moon. It was a new feeling, absolutely without focus for him" (113). *Fire* does not state and then enforce a thesis, advancing a conclusion from the beginning and then supporting it. Instead Mailer notes each stage of an ongoing process and each point in the ebb and flow of emotion.

Mailer is telling this story after it has happened. He is not in fact spontaneous as a persona. He is recounting his effort in the past. Yet there is still a sense of spontaneity and simultaneity. Rather than start from the standpoint of what he has learned after all is said and done, he begins at the beginning, recording his first impression and then the second, then the third and fourth, as well as the principle of movement that emerges as he changes. The overall structure of the book suggests this progressive revision. Each of the three parts is a different approach to the same material, as if Mailer starts over three times and offers us three different versions of the same book—the first, "Aquarius," an account of his writing of the piece; the second, "Apollo," a more conventional, journalistic account of the mission itself; the third, "The Age of Aquarius," a poetic meditation on what the mission in the end might mean. The three parts of the book seem to be deliberately redundant and overlapping—and each section is progressively tighter and more synthetic, an increasingly more satisfying mastering of the material, the contradictions and loose ends more crafted and under control with each attempt.

We have seen the spontaneity implied in the rhythms of Wolfe's language. The image Wolfe offers us is of the excited journalist typing madly through the night under the influence of a sublime subject, his thinking and his writing simultaneous. The process

Mailer dramatizes is more deliberate, slower, more measured. He ruminates. He broods. And he is more explicit in his recording of the process, calling attention to himself as a writer in the act of composing. What Mailer offers us in every passage of *Fire* is a record of his thinking at that particular moment in his struggle to understand the implications of the moon landing:

> Now was there to be a future science of death, or did death (like smell and sound and time—like the theory of the dream) resist all scientists, navigators, nomenclature and charts and reside in the realm of such unanswerables as whether the cause of cancer was a malfunction of the dream? *Did* the souls of the dead choose to rise? Was the thought of expiring on the moon an abyss of unpleasantness because the soul must rest in the tombless vacuums of a torso dead on the moon and therefore not able to voyage toward its star? A vertigo of impressions, but Aquarius had been living at the edge of such thoughts for years. It was possible there was nothing more important in a man's life than the hour and the route and the power of his death, yes, certainly if his death were to launch him into another kind of life. And the astronauts—of this he was convinced—would think this way, or at least would have that vein of imagination in some inviolate and noncommunicatory circuit of their brain; somewhere, far below the language of their communication, they must suspect that the gamble of a trip to the moon and back again, if carried off in all success, might give thrust for some transpostmortal insertion to the stars. Varoom! Last of all over the years had Aquarius learned how to control the rapid acceleration of his brain. (35)

The structure of these sentences reflects the spontaneous ebbs and flows of rapid thought: the parenthetical additions, the dashes, the "and's" added on to a sentence apparently finished but now opened up again, the "yes" inserted as if to confirm an original intuition. Questions lead to more questions. The effect is to suggest "the rapid acceleration of his brain," including his own second awareness ("Varoom!") of that acceleration. Looking back from the vantage of tranquil recollection, Mailer shares with us his original spontaneous overflow. He is thinking aloud, and his interest is in portraying what he later calls "the style of his thought" (150).

Mailer's frequent discussions about his problems and choices composing the book are even more explicitly metadiscursive. Rather than write about his subject, he writes about his writing about the subject. "There were assignments which could make a reporter happy," he tells us at one such juncture, political conventions, for example, or championship fights. "Give Aquarius a great heavyweight championship fight, and he would give you a two-volume work. There was so much to say." But the task of writing about the moon landing is qualitatively different. "The only thing open was the technology—the participants were so overcome by the magnitude of their venture they seemed to consider personal motivation as somewhat obscene" (105).

Earlier he devotes a long passage to discussing the problems of doing his "homework for space" and reporting on a process "too complex to be reported for daily news stories by passing observers" (88). And he goes on to discuss in detail his own strategies as a reporter—why, for example, he chooses to write about himself as an individual rather than concentrate on the astronauts. The frame thus impinges on the picture. The process of writing the book becomes the subject of the book. It's as if we are constantly being brought backstage to watch the scenery being replaced and the booms lowered, the actors dressed in costume.

In all these ways Mailer is responding to the problem of the ineffable. If discourse is impossible, metadiscourse results, language turning away from its inexplicable object and back onto itself. Or to put this another way, the actual demonstration of Mailer's subject is impossible: the emphasis thus naturally shifts to the subject of the writer and his relationship to the audience, the other two poles within the economy of the rhetorical triangle. This is precisely Mailer's analysis of his rhetorical situation. The experience of the moon shot, he says, is "almost impossible to write about" because of its peculiar complexity. His colleagues in the press must struggle to write stories understandable to the general public; their approach is direct, conventional journalism, the effort to assimilate the facts and then report the objective reality of what they see. But Mailer realizes that "in dealing with men who were enormously complex or with men whose passions were buried in the depths of their work," conventional journalistic technique—the interview, for instance—"could be misleading." In the end it is more informative to dwell on the responses of a single representative individual, detailing the complex reactions of the writer himself, even if his experience might appear contradictory or might take place on the edges of the event (88–89). He will "approach" the astronauts "via Aquarius" (4).

Notice the structure of this passage itself: first the claim that the experience is inexplicable, then the metadiscursive discussion of why Mailer can't approach the experience directly. The inexplicable displaces discourse and generates metadiscourse.

Mailer makes the case more forcefully in *The Armies of the Night*. It may be questionable, he admits, to write an "intimate history" of the March on the Pentagon, a history focusing on the experience of a single, possibly peripheral participant, but "for this historian there is no other choice." The March on the Pentagon is "an ambiguous event whose essential value or absurdity may not be established for ten or twenty years, or indeed ever." Thus, "to place the real principals, the founders or designers of the March, men like David Dellinger, or Jerry Rubin, in the center of our portrait could prove misleading." It is more accurate and more revealing in the end to concentrate on the ambiguous character of Mailer himself. As a "figure of monumental disproportions" he serves as "the bridge." Through him we can "recapture the precise feel of the ambiguity of the event" (67–68).

The structure of *Armies* is identical to *Fire*. Here again Mailer defines America as "apocalyptic," a "tender mysterious bitch whom no one would ever know" (114). Here again he chooses an event representative of the American dichotomy, both America's underlying human power and its momentum towards technological apocalypse. In the March on the Pentagon, he thinks, America had once again "begun to partake of Mystery," tapping into its power, drawing on the energy of protest and revolutionary imagination Mailer finds lacking in the complacent middle class. Yet as event it comes to represent as well a generation of young minds raised on plastic and interchangeable mechanical parts. On both levels the roots of the experience are "undiscoverable" (103)—

Armies is an effort to brood and ruminate about "the mysterious character" of "a quintessentially American event" (216). And the shape of that brooding is metadiscursive. In the face of an event that defies easy synthesis or final formulation, Mailer turns to recounting his own effort to understand the event. Again there is extensive discourse about the writing of the discourse. Again there is the recording of mood, the telling of a developing insight. Again there is the apparent autobiography, Mailer writing about Mailer. As he remarks in *Cannibals and Christians*, alluding to a turning point in his conception of the novel, "I think I must have felt at that time as if I would never be able to write in the third person until I developed a coherent view of life. I don't know that I've been able to altogether" (209).

II

In a long pseudoplatonic dialogue in *Cannibals and Christians* Mailer chooses the curious image of driftwood to figure this notion of form. Driftwood, he says, "is a fine form. It expresses the essence of form." In its textures and surfaces we see what "proved most dear to the wood, what resisted decomposition the longest, what—if we know to read it—was saved by accident, what was etched by design. The form of driftwood is the record of a siege." Form in general, he goes on—shifting the metaphor again—is "the record of a war." "It is the record, as seen in a moment of rest" (369–70). What driftwood figures in this cryptic pronouncement is the idea of process. Driftwood reveals after the fact the buffets and blows of the random waves, its drift, its randomness. Form records the process of the author trying to come to terms with an experience, embodying each moment, each engagement and falling back, in that constant interaction with a meaning. It is a *record*, not a result, not a summary or distillation.

Moreover, one consequence of embodying the process of thought is an emphasis on the actions of the perceiving self. What form records is the self in its transactions with the world—thus autobiography, thus Mailer stepping back to feature himself in the search for meaning. Form, he says still later in this dialogue, is the "record of a relationship," the relationship, he implies, between the writer and his material (372).

Implicit in this war is the difficulty of bringing the material under control. The effort of form is a battle because the subject exceeds or nearly exceeds the possibilities of ordering: "Form is the record of every intent of the soul to express itself upon another soul or spirit, its desire to reveal the shape—which is to say the *mystery* of the time it contains in itself" (369–73). For Mailer form is a record of the writer's effort to express a mystery. It is the representation of the process because the product is finally inexplicable. As Richard Poirier observes of this passage, "the definition of form emerges not as a static proposition but as something jogged into meaning, now by one, now by another contributory suggestion," just as in the dialogue itself Mailer records the relationship between the speakers, "a relationship that partakes also of the strife, the argumentative resistance out of which form emerges" (14–15). Metaphor itself in Mailer's aesthetic is a record of process: "a metaphor is a relation," Mailer says. "It changes as our experience changes" (*Cannibals* 168). Like the metaphor of driftwood in the dialogue, which becomes then an image of war, change, relationship in turn, metaphors in Mailer's writing are meant as points of departures rather than fixed images. Tenors change and evolve as Mailer discovers the unfolding implications of the vehicle.

Part of what Mailer records of this process is his own failure. In *Fire* he repeatedly calls attention to his inability to encompass the sublimity of his object. Standing in the Vehicle Assembly Building he feels "*his* mighty ego" dwarfed and overwhelmed and for a moment almost obliterated. He begins to observe the experience "without an ego," "as if he were invisible" (55–57). The subject of the space project daunts and even changes him. "It was a terror to write if one wished to speak of important matters and did not know if one was qualified," he says. "To write was to judge, and Aquarius may never have tried a subject which tormented him so" (435–36). That torment is manifest in every convoluted, metadiscursive phrase in the book, in the repeated attempts to approach the psychology of the astronauts, now this way, now that, in the apparent struggle to shape an argument and discover an appropriate form. At one point he even confesses a desire to give up: "He who had once thought he had only to get on all the radio and television available and he would be able to change the world, now wished only to flee this room with its hundreds of journalists, some so bored and aimless they even wished to interview him, he who now had nothing to say" (107).

But in Mailer even more than in Wolfe and Capote, these claims are figurative, poses that are themselves the appropriate form they claim to be lacking. The figure depends on the disjunction between Mailer's "mighty ego" and his inability to word the wordless: if he, with his great powers and his great pretensions, is stymied by the space program, how complex and powerful that subject must be. It is on this level that Mailer acts out the rhetoric of the sublime. In fact, whereas the negative logic of sublimity is only implicit in Wolfe and Capote, Mailer seems to be deliberately and formally engaging in the rhetoric of the sublime. He makes explicit his failure, makes deliberate the enactment of failure as a way of figuring his subject. What appears to be a displacement, then, comes to serve the ends of representation and presence: the failure to signify signifies. Or to borrow a phrase from *Armies*, Mailer "converts [his] deficiency to an asset"—"From gap to gain," after all, "is very American" (44).

This is the source of Armstrong's power as a speaker and public figure for Mailer. "At communicating he was as tight as a cramped muscle," yet "perversely, it became his most impressive quality." It's as if "what was best in the man was most removed from the surface, so valuable that it must be protected by a hundred reservations" (30). The very disparity between surface and depth is an index to Armstrong's potential heroism. Gap becomes gain because, in the negative logic of the sublime, it signals greatness beyond words.

More importantly, it would be wrong to see Mailer as passive in any way in *Fire* or in *Armies*. While he concedes difficulty and acknowledges limits, resignation is only an occasional and uncharacteristic mood. The dominant mood for Mailer is combat.

His record is of a war. He shares the combativeness of the press corps as it struggles to wring any feeling or humanity from the astronauts in their preflight news conferences. With each question about the possibility of death or the importance of the mission for the world, the astronauts became more stubbornly taciturn and utilitarian, disavowing the emotional. And as the press conference wears on, the writers become "a little weary" and, in fact, even antagonistic. "The questions began to have a new tone, an edge, the subtlest quivering suggestion that intellectual contempt was finally a weapon not to be ignored." "Covertly, the mood of a hunt was on." The battle is between the technological and the poetic, the mechanical and the passionate, the impersonal and the personal, and Mailer's allegiances are unmistakable: "Were these astronauts not much more than brain-programmed dolts?" Unlike Wolfe, Mailer isn't trying to be an insider here. This is the crucial difference between *Fire* and *The Right Stuff*. Mailer is not trying to see through the astronauts' eye sockets, not using their jargon, adopting their mannerisms. Instead he puts himself on the outside of the experience from the beginning, setting himself up in opposition to the astronauts and then repeatedly calling attention to that opposition. The press conference is a battle: "the writers were pushing Armstrong now" (37, 41).

The magnitude of the moon shot may push against Mailer's ego, yet at the same time he is "pushing and shoving on it" (55). The pressure comes from the outside, impinging on Mailer's sensibility; yet it also comes from Mailer himself as he asserts the powers of his language against the material at hand. As he puts it in *Armies*, "no recognition existed of the existence of anything beyond the range of his reach" (24). He may fail in the effort to word the wordless, but he is always trying to extend his range. Writing for him is like pole-vaulting, he explains in *Cannibals and Christians*. "The man who wins is the man who jumps highest without knocking off the bar. And a man who clears the stick with precise form but eighteen inches below the record commands less of our attention" (108).

Mailer's language here of "pushing" and straining evokes the metaphor I developed for Wolfe. Like Wolfe, Mailer pushes the outside of the envelope of language, straining to the limits of expression in an effort to reach the level of the wordless. Metadiscourse, like rhetorical intensification, is a kind of pushing against the limits of language, a stretching and expanding of the medium. But at the same time Mailer is pushing back against forces he seems to think are pushing in on him from the outside. The inside/outside distinction that the image suggests becomes in Mailer an alternating polarity.

The dialogue on form makes the tension clear: "Don't you see whatever is alive, or intent, or obsessed, must wage an active war: it creates the possibility for form in its environment by its every attempt to shape the environment. Wherever the environment resists, the result is a form. When the soul is mighty and the environment resists mightily, the form is exceptional or extraordinary" (370–71). Mailer is alive, intent, obsessed in *Fire*, and he wages there an active war. Form emerges from the attempt to shape the environment and depends in the end on the resistance of the environment to such shaping. The war in Mailer is not only the effort to push back against the forces threatening language from the outside but more than that an effort to encompass this radical otherness, to enclose it, claim it, in language.

III

In *The Armies of the Night* the nature and the significance of this war becomes even clearer—and not only for Mailer, but for Wolfe and Capote as well. Because its subject is rhetoric itself, *Armies* helps us to see still more dramatically why Mailer is waging his war and what the consequences really are if he wins.

Armies is about speechmaking. It dramatizes a series of speeches: the infamous program at the Ambassador Theatre where Mailer steals the show from Goodman and Lowell; the speeches and demonstrations prior to the March on the Pentagon at the First Congregational Church and the Justice Department; the interminable speeches on the day of the march, speeches on the lawn, on the bridge, on the steps of the Pentagon. The action of *Armies*—with the crucial exception of the demonstration itself—is not physical but verbal. As event it is composed of repeated attempts by various people to persuade audiences to action or feeling.

In the process of describing these rhetorical performances, Mailer assumes the role of rhetorical critic. His interpretation of the experience is an interpretation of the success or failure of rhetorical performance—principally the failure. The March on the Pentagon is an opportunity for Mailer to attack the false and dishonest forms of rhetoric which are indicative of the totalitarian, technological plague he has railed against throughout his career. The dissembling, euphemistic, falsely rational rhetoric of the Johnson administration, for example, is for Mailer representative of "the diseases of America, its oncoming totalitarianism, its oppressiveness, its smog" (188). The disparity between the violent, obscene reality of the Vietnam War and the bland technologese of the administration's official justifications is an index to the insanity and self-deception destroying America. In its formulaic indirectness, its use of "nothing but connectives and aggregate words," the rhetoric of the Johnson administration is, to borrow a phrase from *Cannibals and Christians*, "the essence of totalitarian prose": "It does not define, it does not deliver. It oppresses. It obstructs from above. It is profoundly contemptuous of the minds who will receive the message" (51).

But oddly enough, Mailer's primary target in *Armies* is not the rhetoric of the establishment but the rhetoric of the New Left, the instigators of the protest. Repeatedly he attacks what he perceives as the self-indulgent, arid intellectualism of Ivy League, Berkeley radicalism. For him it is too organized, too antiseptic and sterile. In an important chapter, "In the Rhetoric," he identifies the language of the New Left with "the mediocre middle-class middle-aged masses," with "technology land." The problem with Ivy League, professorial protesters is that "they could not conceive of a revolution without hospitals, lawyers, mass meetings, and leaflets to pass out at the polls" (96). In their efforts to organize and speechify, they fail to recognize the concreteness of violence.

Dr. Spock's speech at the Lincoln Memorial, for example, is "about par." It "said almost nothing one had not heard before, but the sentiments were incontestable, and the words went out over the loudspeakers and dropped in dull echoes" (99). Similarly, Paul Goodman's speech on the same occasion is "worthy, humorless, incontrovertible, and not uncourageous," but ultimately ineffective. "Only Goodman could say 'at the present in the world,' 'implement,' 'disastrous policies,' 'overwhelming lobby,' 'expand and rigidify'"—his style "read like LBJ's exercises in Upper Rhetoric (the Rhetoric, Mailer now decided, being located three inches below and back of Erogenous Zone Clitoric)" (98). Goodman and Spock represent, ironically, what Weaver would call the "spaciousness" of an older rhetoric based on sweeping generalizations and shared assumptions.

For years the political faithful had all been "bored by speeches, polemic and political programmings which invariably detailed the sound-as-brick logic of the next step in some hard new Left program" (85). The New Left, like the Old Left, has committed itself to logic and to the working out of problems through rational consensus. Its concern is with establishing premises and following outlines of action. As Mailer listens to speech after speech before and during the March on the Pentagon, he becomes increasingly convinced that such step-by-step, careful, programmatic expression is not only stylistically uninteresting but finally useless. The crowds are all "ground down by words," deadened by "the soul-killing repetition of political jargon" (102). No one listens. Spacious rhetoric fails. The cheers of the audience were "like the bored sounds a baseball crowd makes when their side gets a walk and it no longer matters very much because the team is far ahead. So was everyone here now far ahead on Rhetoric" (99–100). Over and over again what Mailer recounts is the failure of language to unify or persuade: microphones don't work; crowds mill about or chant slogans, oblivious to what's being said on stage; everywhere there is a mood of excitement and confrontation which renders language beside the point.

As Edward Corbett observes in an important article of this time, "The Rhetoric of the Closed Hand and the Rhetoric of the Open Fist," demonstrations are necessary only after accommodations in language become impossible. Physical demonstrations like marches and sit-ins are fundamentally nonverbal, a testimony to the inadequacy of language. Booth suggests that the sixties were a time of rhetorical crisis, of shouting and sloganizing in which protesters assumed that rational discussion about right reasons was fruitless and deluding. The practical world of protest and response, he says, resembles "a world of futile babblers": "Passionate commitment has lost its connection with the provision of good reasons. And reason has been reduced to logical calculation and proof about whatever does not matter enough to engage commitment" (*Modern Dogma* xi). As Mailer puts it, "rhetoric hand in hand with reason put no spirit of war into revolutionary boys" (264–65).

The confrontation at the Pentagon, after all, is fundamentally silent. In *Armies* it is figured by silence. Suddenly the speeches and even the shouting die away and Mailer finds himself standing a few feet from a line of federal marshals who resolutely refuse to speak: "They were out there waiting. Two moods confronted one another, two separate senses of a private silence" (129). Mailer's description of his arrest is appropriately concrete and stark, free of self-reflexive commentary: "he made a point of stepping neatly and decisively over the low rope"; "the MP lifted his club to his chest"; "He had a quick impression of hard-faced men with gray eyes burning some transparent fuel for flame" (129–30). The rhetoric and the rhetorical criticism give way here to hard-edged narrative. The moment is silent, nonverbal, a moment of action.

Throughout *Armies* Mailer is strongly attracted to the realities and concreteness of physical action in the world. In his rejection of spacious rhetoric, he is compelled by the mythic and heroic proportions of the march as physical rather than verbal demonstration. There is in the character of Mailer in this book an anti-intellectualism and an antiverbal bias not unlike that of Kesey in *Acid Test*.

The fact that Mailer participates in the march to begin with is an indication that on one level at least he chooses action over words. Moreover, his justifications for participating emphasize the failure or irrelevancy of language and the need for action. He and Macdonald and Lowell do not need to "talk and argue" about the march. They leave the programs and the rationalization for the

Left. They know that if the march succeeds it will be "as a result of episodes one had never anticipated." They trust to the recalcitrance and complexity of experience. "One did not march on the Pentagon and look to get arrested as a link in a master scheme." One marches for primitive, intuitive reasons, reasons of passion, the heart; one marches for instinct, not intellect: "One marched on the Pentagon because . . . because . . . and here the reasons became so many and so curious and so vague, so political and so primitive, that there was no need, or perhaps no possibility to talk about it yet, one could only ruminate over the morning coffee" (86). For Mailer the march is an opportunity to come into contact with the great power and mystery of the American experience, a mystery that is by definition beyond language, which requires action, physical presence, rather than verbal formulae. What he shares with the marchers is an "unspoken happy confidence that politics had again become mysterious, had begun to partake of Mystery; that gave life to a thought the gods were back in human affairs" (86).The talk is over; now is the time for the purity of action. Even within this statement there is silence—as recorded in the ellipses—the suspension of language in anticipation of action.

Standing on the lawn as the protesters gather for the march, Mailer feels an intoxicating sense of pending battle. The sensation is felt in the blood. "The morning was so splendid—it spoke of a vitality in nature which no number of bombings in space nor inner-space might ever subdue." The costumes, the sheer physical presence of so many thousands, the excited murmuring and laughing, all "spoke of future redemptions as quickly as they reminded of hog-swillings from the past, and the thin air! wine of Civil War apples in the October air! edge of excitement and awe" (93). Here again is the sublime. Mailer is moved by the spectacle of the march. Like the space program on one level, the march symbolizes for him the realm of poetry and power versus the domain of "the technicians, bureaucrats, and labor leaders who ran the governmental military industrial complex of super-technology land" (94). He is intoxicated by feeling, by the "beat of a primitive drum," by the "incredible spectacle now gathering—tens of thousands traveling hundreds of miles to attend a symbolic battle." His language is exclamatory, celebratory, not argumentative or demonstrative. It is an apostrophe to America.

But if Mailer chooses at the moment of the march to war rather than argue, if he finds himself committed in that moment to "revolutionary aesthetics" and the "primitive" power of symbolic action, if he even claims a "final allegiance" with "the villains who were hippies" (94), he nonetheless later chooses to write a book about the experience. The engagement in action is in the past; it is the writing of the book that is present. The book is not the action but an interpretation of it after the fact. Mailer acts. His action in the march clearly validates, and is meant to validate, his later language. But in a more important way his language validates the action. Ultimately, Mailer's allegiances are with words, with language—with rhetoric.

What disturbs Mailer about the protest movement, despite his realization that protest has become necessary, is the underlying disorder of the demonstration. Washington on the eve of the march is "not in focus" (11). The march is disorganized, chaotic, without a "center," its fifty thousand participants "unaffiliated or disaffiliated" (11–12). The "protean forms" of protest cause him "anxiety," he admits (57). The vague and sophomoric bombast of the movement's public documents are an index to the problem. Ironically, despite the commitment of the Left to the logic of the next step, their pamphlets and proclamations in the heat of the moment are merely declaratory and assertive, not demonstrative or logical (58–59). One pamphlet contradicts or undercuts another; there seems to be no unifying logic in the distribution of leaflets. Mailings, programs, manifestos, requests for money bulge from a folder in Mailer's attache case, each issued by a different revolutionary committee or subcommittee (usually designated by some obscure acronym), each proclaiming the need for action in its own hyperbolic terms. It is unclear who is in charge or what the plan of action will be.

While the march is close to the wellsprings of American power and mystery, it is also associated in Mailer's mind with McLuhanesque media brainwashing: the young people participating in the march have been "galvanized into surrealistic modes of response by commercials cutting into dramatic narratives, and parents flipping from network to network." They have been "forced willynilly to build their idea of the space-time continuum (and therefore their nervous system) on the jumps and cracks and leaps and breaks which every phenomenon from the media seemed to contain within it" (87). Raised on television, the protesters seem unable to use language clearly or consistently. They expect immediate gratification, depend on the total assimilation of impression or information afforded by images.

And underneath this anxiety about the nonverbal, even antiverbal predisposition of the marchers and the march itself is Mailer's understanding that the protest could actually result in violence. Unlike the other, more naïve, "week-end revolutionaries," Mailer is not sanguine about the possibility of having his head split open. "The thought of mace in his hard-used eyes," he says drolly, "inspired a small horror" (56). Later he acknowledges more soberly that though he and his fellow protesters were "hardly in the mood for further addresses" as they approach the Pentagon, "combat was getting nearer—one could tell by the slow contractions of the gut." The opposition is between violence and language, and at this point Mailer chooses words, if only temporarily: "The idea of listening to speeches was not intolerable" on the brink of genuine conflict (117).

At several points Mailer is quite explicit about the opposition I'm suggesting. "Actually," he says, "he had hated the thought of signing the protest, he had piped up every variety of the extraordinarily sound argument that his work was the real answer to Vietnam, and these mass demonstrations, sideshows, and bloody income tax protests just took energy and *money* away from the real thing—getting the work out" (58). Sideshows and mass demonstrations are fundamentally antithetical to Mailer as a writer. They do not produce aesthetically pleasing or worthwhile work. Impatient with Goodman earlier in the week, he asks, "When was everyone going to cut out the nonsense and get to work, do their own real work? One's own literary work was the only answer to the war in Vietnam" (9). Mailer's faith is in language as protest. His identity as narrator in *Armies* is fundamentally that of the writer, or as he frequently calls himself, the "Novelist," and in this role he has to see the protest from the very beginning as inimical to his own interests.

But Mailer's allegiances to language are most evident not in any explicit statements he makes but rather in the nature and movement of his own language and rhetoric.

His speechmaking as master of ceremony at the Ambassador is evidently an example of his failure as an orator. He makes a fool out of himself: strutting on stage doing adolescent impersonations of Cassius Clay or Lyndon Johnson, shouting obscenities at the audience, threatening his fellow speakers. "Come on, Norman, say something," a member of the audience shouts back as Mailer stumbles and rants. He is caught off balance when de Grazia replaces him as MC in the beginning of the evening, and from then on he is out of control, antagonistic and angry. Like MacDonald and Lowell, we are meant to be embarrassed by the spectacle.

But at the same time this clearly rhetorical moment—which Mailer develops at great length in the first third of *Armies*—suggests Mailer's extraordinary rhetorical self-consciousness, his awareness of the effects of language and his commitment to passionate rhetorical speech. Mailer finds himself "happy" right before he is to go on stage, invigorated by the prospect of speaking before an audience. "Like all good professionals, he was stimulated by the chance to try a new if related line of work." As a writer he finds in public speaking an opportunity to discover new powers of language. "The pleasure of speaking in public was the sensitivity it offered: with every phrase one was better or worse, close or less close to the existential promise of truth . . . which hovers on good occasions like a presence between speaker and audience" (29). Yes, he repeats several pages later, "The Beast was in a great good mood. He was soon to speak; that was food for all" (30). He fancies himself in fact a "fair country orator, for he loved to speak, he loved in fact to holler, and liked to hear a crowd holler back" (36).

The rhetoric Mailer espouses on this occasion is a rhetoric of spontaneity and risk. Just as "a good half of writing consists of being sufficiently sensitive to the moment to reach for the next promise which is usually hidden in some word or phrase just a shift to the side of one's conscious intent," in public speaking "one had to trick or seize or submit to the grace of each moment," moments which are often "occasions of some mystery" when "consciousness and grace come together" (28). Mailer thus walks onto stage without "any idea of what he would say," his mind "empty" (36). He improvises, making things up as he goes in response to his instincts about audience mood and approval, counting on "the bonus" of some apt phrase or word but willing to suffer the consequences of temporary bumbling and failure (37).

Yet at the same time Mailer's rhetoric is deliberately artificial and calculated. Throughout this long and disastrous evening, Mailer is remarkably sensitive to the responses of the audience, carefully recording every burst of laughter, applause, every titter, every sense of mood and shift of mood: "cries of laughter came back. A very small pattern of applause" or "confused titters, small reaction" or "wild yells and chills of silence from different reaches of the crowd" (36–38). With his "orator's ear" he records the ebb and flow of response, calculating how the audience will react to each new obscenity or rhetorical lunge. His narrative of this event is an intricate record, almost a scripting, of statement and response, statement and response.

Spontaneity itself, apparent lack of artifice, even awkwardness and foolishness, Mailer realizes, can have important rhetorical consequences. His plan is to confess that he was late for his appearance as MC because he had to pee on the floor of the dark men's room, and thus—to return to a phrase we considered earlier—convert a "deficiency to an asset." After all, "From gap to gain is very American":

> While the audience was recovering from the existential anxiety of encountering an orator who confessed to such a crime, he would be able—their attention now riveted—to bring them up to a contemplation of deeper problems, of, indeed, the deepest problems, the most chilling alternatives, and would from there seek to bring them back to a restorative view of man. Man might be a fool who peed in the wrong pot, man was also a scrupulous servant of the self-damaging admission; man was therefore a philosopher who possessed the magic stone;

he could turn loss to philosophical gain, and so illumine the deeps. (31–32)

Turning loss to philosophical gain is the rhetorical principle throughout Mailer's performance. When he steps away from the microphone and bellows to the audience that he would rather shout than be victimized by technology, Mailer is disassociating himself from the artificial and proclaiming himself honest and sincere. In Perelman's terms, he is implicitly establishing a "philosophical pair" between appearance and reality, then claiming the authority of the real for himself. "Elements which can be interpreted as indications of spontaneity are particularly efficacious for ensuring correspondence with reality, and, accordingly, for aiding persuasion" (455). As Cicero puts it, a speaker "should . . . avoid, so to speak, cementing his words together too smoothly, for the hiatus and clash of vowels has something agreeable about it and shows a not unpleasant carelessness on the part of a man who is paying more attention to thought than to words" (*Orator* 363). Spontaneity signals openness; gap becomes gain because the audience can identify with the struggling of the all too human speaker. By dramatizing himself as comic fool, Mailer tries to secure identifications which can then lead to higher orders of thought. Fundamentally, the rhetoric of spontaneity is a strategy of ethos.

Mailer's other apparently antirhetorical gestures also are meant to achieve rhetorical ends. He insults his audience, calling them "dead-heads," for example, or questioning their real philosophical understanding of what they are about to do in the March on the Pentagon. His goal is obviously to "awaken" his listeners and shock them out of complacency. Prior to his entrance, as Mac-Donald and the others speak, he notices that the audience is "stricken, inert, unable to rise to a word the speaker is offering them." Only rhetorical "dynamite"—insults, taunts—can "bring life" (33–34). Obscenity serves the same function, and something more. Although "shit" and "fuck" are not the conventional words of argumentation, Mailer means them to express his rage at easy rationalizations and his impatience with passive intellectualism. The concreteness of obscenity, its earthiness, is meant as a challenge to the logic-of-the-next step and its abstractions from the real world of experience.

In all this Mailer invokes the metaphor of battle, recalling for us his description of form as the record of a war. *Armies* is obviously involved in the symbolism of battle for Mailer, but in the end the battle is not between the protesters and the establishment but between word and listener, word and meaning, word and chaos. He holds his opening remarks in "close file in his mind like troops ranked in order before the parade"; he fires "apocalyptic salvos," makes "oratorical charges"; he seeks to "drive away some sepulchral phantoms of a variety which inhabited the profound middle-class schist," then "charge the center of vested spookery." The circumstances of this speech, he says, are clearly "military" (32, 35, 37, 38, 40). As he improvises in front of the audience, he struggles to "live on the edge of that rhetorical sword he would soon try to run through the heart of the audience." The rhetoric of spontaneity is also the rhetoric of battle, and Mailer's purposes, it is clear, are rhetorical. His speech does fail in the end. The applause is only "fair. Not weak, but empty of large demonstration" (51). MacDonald undercuts the peformance entirely when he remarks that he couldn't "hear a word" of what Mailer said because of the terrible acoustics (52). Yet our impression after this scene is of Mailer as warring rhetor intent on victory over the audience, and ultimately over unmeaning.

Just as importantly, Mailer engages in argument, deliberation—in rhetoric in its classical, Aristotelian sense—in the text of *Armies* itself, and not the impulsive, failed deliberation of the Ambassador Theatre but a more reasoned, calm, retrospective deliberation. He deliberates in writing, in the sanity and quiet of the study, not in the heat of the moment on a stage in front of a live and restless audience. Although he rejects the sound-as-a-brick logical rhetoric of the next step, Mailer is not hesitant about marshalling evidence and advancing premises himself, particularly in his long and calculated argument against the Vietnam War. His argument easily submits itself to a topical analysis: "All wars were bad which undertook daily operations which burned and bombed large numbers of women and children; all wars were bad which relocated populations . . . all wars were bad which had no line of battle or discernible climax . . . Certainly any war was a bad war which required an inability to reason as the price of retaining one's patriotism" (185). Mailer here argues through definition, and the definition depends on the relationship between the war and its bad results. As in all pragmatic arguments, "from the moment a fact-consequence connection is apparent, the argumentation is valid, whatever the merits of the connection itself" (Perelman 267). Implicit is the abbreviated syllogism: if the war leads to these consequences, and if these consequences are bad, the war is bad. From another perspective such a syllogism depends on the "argument of waste," since what Mailer emphasizes is the uselessness of the war. "A good war," he says, "like anything else which is good, offers the possibility that further effort will produce a determinable effect upon chaos, evil, or waste." Since the Vietnam War does not order chaos or produce any determinable effect on evil, it is itself a waste and therefore wrong.

Mailer also relies here on the rhetoric of reiteration to magnify the presence of these arguments. Each declaration repeats the structure of the original sentence: all wars are bad which . . . , all wars are bad which . . . , and so on. Indeed, every use of rhetorical figures or sentence rhythms for the purposes of magnification marks Mailer as a rhetorician. From this perspective nearly every sentence in *Armies* is rhetorical, an attempt through style to create effects in the readers' sensibility.

Mailer engages in similar kinds of deliberation throughout *Armies*. The form of his ruminations is an internal debate about the cancer eating away at America. Repeatedly he interrupts the narrative to offer short "diatribes" against the debasement of language, the debasement of love, the failure to communicate. All that we have been exploring in Mailer's fairly explicit theories of language and its relation to culture in America is ultimately in the form of deliberation. It is rhetorical. More important than the arguments themselves in all these cases is the fact of argument, the presence of the "therefores" and "thens," the fact of the premises and the structure of the deductions and inferences that follow from them. Ironically, Mailer's language is in many ways as "spacious" as the ineffective rhetorical gestures he attacks.

But even this is to limit the notion of rhetoric too much. Rhetoric includes not simply deliberation but information. *Armies* is principally and from the beginning an attempt to *inform* the broad American reading public about a significant cultural and political event. Mailer's rhetorical motive is not simply to venture his own arguments about left-conservatism or the insanity of the war but in a deeper sense to explain an important experience to his audience, and thus to make sense out of the experience. It is on this level that *Armies* is on the side of rhetoric and language.

Mailer informs and inteprets in the role of the Ruminator. After the fact of the experience, he reflects and broods over its meaning. As in his meditations on the bus on the way to jail, his thoughts "meander" "down a long broad slow river of thought," and the form of his discourse is the form of that meandering. As "shopping streets flickered past the bus window," Mailer's thinking "eddies" through "a melancholy which was not without its private flavor, for he felt remarkably disembodied from all proceedings" (158). There are no definitive meanings here. Mailer is dramatizing himself at the moment of thinking, sharing the coming to conclusions, the act, rather than the conclusions themselves. The river is a river of thought, not of simple emotion, certainly not of action. The language is an attempt to discover meaning—and the attempt itself is a meaning. It asserts the possibility of thought and order even if it fails to find definitive answers. Its shape is the shape of an intellect. Its language is measured and slow and broad.

From the beginning of *Armies* Mailer's voice resembles that of the old-fashioned Victorian narrator, intrusive, almost scholarly and pedantic: "From the outset," he says in the very first sentence of the book, "let us bring you news of your protagonist. The following is from *Time* magazine, October 27, 1967." The use of citation, the awareness of reader, the somewhat pompous inclusion of the audience in the pronoun "we," all project an impression of control and formality and even fastidiousness. "Now we may leave *Time* in order to find out what happened," he says after the quotation. This is not the voice of the demonstrator but of the lecturer, the pedant.

In the next chapter Mailer's sentences seem to deliberately check the advancement of the plot. As readers we expect the narrator to begin a description of the action, yet instead Mailer dwells on his refusal to pick up the telephone. For several paragraphs he details his complex attitudes toward interrupting his work and wasting time in conversation, and for the duration of this block we are suspended in time: the phone is ringing, but Mailer steps out of time to digress; we are suspended prior to the moment of his answering the phone:

> He had an answer service, a secretary, and occasional members of his family to pick up the receiver for him—he discouraged his own participation on the phone—sometimes he would not even speak to old friends. Touched by faint intimations of remorse, he would call them back later. He had the idea—it was undeniably oversimple—that if you spent too much time on the phone in the evening, you destroyed some kind of creativity for the dawn. (It was taken for granted that nothing respectable would come out of the day if the morning began on the phone, and indeed for periods when he was writing he looked on transactions via telephone as Arabs look upon pig.) (4–5)

No sentence is allowed to advance without interruption. It's not just that Mailer chooses to dwell on this mundane psychic event. Even here he refuses to simply describe what he feels. He must interrupt and modify, digress, check the movement of his first impulse. Each sentence becomes increasingly recursive, each interjection and parenthesis not only longer but also more digressive, demanding more independent interest (as "Arabs look upon pigs" is not a simile we easily pass over). And this is not the diction of action: "transactions," "undeniably," "privacies," "promiscuous," "psychic equivalent of static." The language is conservative, professorial. The image Mailer is trying to project is that of the middle-aged father worried about the moral conduct of his daughter in her freshman year at Barnard, this in sharp contrast to the adolescent, drunken rebel depicted in the *Time* magazine blurb.

The form of this passage thus mirrors its theme: the conflict between writing and action, meditation and the picking up of the phone. The language is as writerly as Mailer's preoccupations. And this conflict continues throughout the book. The voice of the pedant—an irreverent pedant, to be sure, an earthy, provocative professor as it turns out, but an intellectual nonetheless—tells the story of this revolutionary act throughout the book. The strategy is repeatedly to check, slow down through reflection, digression, association, musing, the progress of the plot, the development of action.

There is always a disjunction in Mailer, very Wordsworthian in fact, between present experience and future value. Even at the moment of the confrontation at the Pentagon, at the moment of action and battle, Mailer is anticipating the chance to write about the moment later, to commit it to words and thus understand it. He is always "banking the value" of present experience for future withdrawals in language (160). It would take him "weeks to comprehend this March, and the events now taking place" (192). "There was an explanation to the attack on the Pentagon. It was somewhere in the shape of this event. If only he could brood on it" (199). Implicit in these statements is Mailer's desire to brood. He seems to want to have an experience only so that he can later brood over it and then write about it. The "Mailer" who is protagonist and comic hero of the narrative is a man of experience, but Mailer as writer invests his real authority in the voice of the narrator in the present trying to comprehend the significance of what the comic hero experienced. His action is not the march itself but the effort to "elucidate the mysterious character of that quintessentially American event" (216).

IV

Mailer's rhetoric does not abstract from experience or assert easy slogans. It is concrete, tentative, personal, passionate, embodying process and mystery. Unlike the rhetoricians of the Left or of the Johnson administration, he does not put his arguments in the passive or take them out of their rich and recalcitrant context. Rather than summarize and generalize, he tells the story of his effort to understand, and in all its stubborn, even embarrassing detail. He tells us where he was, in what particular scene and time, when he first had a particular thought, then how that thought was modified, compromised, tested. He grounds his theory in himself as representative figure. He resists the technological impulse to eradicate mystery—or obscure it—by claiming final answers. He acknowledges that the mystery remains beyond his grasp in the end, that there is mystery. His rhetoric is honest because it shows all phases of thought and action, including its embarrassments and reversals. It is therefore complex. It does not, therefore, falsify like the rhetoric of the New Left.

The *Time* blurb Mailer excerpts in the beginning of *Armies* tells the whole story of his experience in the march, summarizing and distilling that complex event into a few short, easily processed paragraphs. The language is full of easy tag phrases and journalistic clichés: "Washington's scruffy Ambassador Theater," "slurping liquor from a coffee mug," "When hecklers mustered the temerity," and so on. The phrases do not trouble us or invite us to dwell on them as phrases. Rather, they serve the ends of easy readability: the sentences are short and punchy, the phrases droll, mildly satiric. We are never checked in our progress to the end of the blurb.

Mailer's language in the next chapter works against readability. Each sentence seems to send out lines of force and influence which work against the next sentence, setting up ripples and currents which move in opposing directions. The tone is difficult to measure, the voice difficult to place or trust. Where *Time* encourages us to accept a kind of easy, false authority, Mailer forces us to question authority. Where *Time* invites us to read to the end without pausing or second thinking, Mailer's piling up of obscure and even arcane metaphors, his use of words which give conflicting signals in the same phrase or comparison, force us to dwell on the surface of language and thus to contemplate the complexity of the experiences it seeks to describe.

From this perspective Mailer's rhetorical performance is in keeping with the definition of rhetoric in the new rhetorical theorists—theorists who are responding to precisely the same problem that Mailer describes in *Armies*. What Mailer means by the "novel," theorists like Booth and Perelman and even Weaver mean by "rhetoric." In their view rhetoric takes place in the context of human interchange and actual experience. Aristotle, of course, establishes that the premises of rhetorical syllogisms "may lie this way or that; for men deliberate and raise questions about things they do, and human actions all belong to this class of uncertainties or mere probabilities" (12). Perelman and Booth and others celebrate this provisional quality of rhetoric. They maintain that what is provable is unimportant, that the contingent, the debatable, and the unprovable encompass all that we value in our daily experience. Their project, developed principally in the sixties, is to re-establish the term "rhetoric" over and against "demonstration" as the term for the humanities.

Ironically, Weaver himself is the most articulate spokesman for this broad definition of rhetoric. "A dialectic takes place in vacuo," he says, but rhetoric "impinges on actuality. That is why rhetoric, with its passion for the actual, is more complete than mere dialectic with its dry understanding. It is more complete on the premise that man is a creature of passion who must live out that passion in the world" (*Language Is Sermonic* 77–78). Whereas demonstration—or logic—divorces the speaker and the audience from consideration of the subject itself, rhetoric is what Burke calls "dramatistic" (*Grammar of Motives* xv–xxiii). Demonstration is concerned only with the content of communication in its most objective form, with the subject of the discourse as it exists apart from the contingency and imprecision—the immeasurability—of feeling and intention. But rhetoric defines reality in terms of that moment when speaker, subject, and audience come together in the concrete act of communication. "It is the very characterizing feature of rhetoric," Weaver says, "that is goes beyond the logical and appeals to other parts of man's constitution, especially to his nature as a pathetic being, that is, a being of feeling and suffering" (*Language Is Sermonic* 205).

It is no accident that much of this rhetoric arose as a response to the failure of rhetoric in the sixties. Booth's *Modern Dogma and the Rhetoric of Assent* is an effort to redefine and salvage rhetoric after the crisis of student protest and demonstration. Young, Becker, and Pike's seminal composition text, *Rhetoric:*

Discovery and Change, also comes out of the political and social conflict of this period, a time when language no longer held out the possibility of genuine accommodation or identification. Mailer's rhetorical performance in *Armies* places him in this same tradition. His effort is finally a defense of rhetoric.

Indeed, only rhetoric understood in this sense can hope to disclose the character of the mystery that is the March on the Pentagon, that is America for Mailer. Experiences of this apocalyptic and even mystical proportion are not approachable through discursive language, or what Perelman calls "demonstration." They are not subject to syllogism. But in its fundamental concreteness, rhetoric can at least suggest what it cannot prove. The subjective, contingent character of rhetoric corresponds to the subjective, contingent character of the experience. Rhetoric can reach the will, the heart, the desire, the source of intuition within us. In Mailer's terms, "the mystery of the events at the Pentagon cannot be developed by the methods of history." The history of such an experience is "interior." The "novel must replace history at precisely that point where experience is sufficiently emotional, spiritual, psychical, moral, existential, or supernatural to expose the fact that the historian in pursuing the experience would be obliged to quit the clearly demarcated limits of historical inquiry" (255). Mailer's opposition is "history" and the "novel," but for our purposes this is identical to the opposition in the new rhetoric between "demonstration" and "argumentation."

In short, for Mailer it is the responsibility of the writer to "educate the nation" (178), and despite his attacks on rhetoric and his attraction to the physical symbol, all the language of *Armies* is directed toward this rhetorical end. Mailer reads the whole recent history of American literature as a struggle with rhetorical responsibility, arguing very much like Weaver against the decline of writing into mere reportage and recording. "The order of magnitude" in the American experience, he writes in *Cannibals and Christians*, challenges literature and language. "It is as if everything changes ten times as fast in America, and this makes for extraordinary difficulty in creating literature" (96). Apocalypse, inexplicability, sublimity strain the expressive capacity of words. The "genteel tradition" in American literature, the novelists of manners like Wharton, Howells, and James, retreat from the vast energies and potentialities of America's central experiences and focus instead on "piety and devotion and style," the "development of taste." Even Hemingway has "given up any desire to be a creation equal to the phenomenon of the country itself." Vision becomes "partial"; the "desire for majesty" is repressed. The novelist no longer even tries to describe the great beast itself but settles for portraying "the paw of the beast" (99).

Against this failure of nerve Mailer opposes the flawed but "heroic" work of Dreiser and Thomas Wolfe, novelists who in his view at least try to capture the "grand" and the "horrible" power of American experience. They attempt to find words for the "future glory and doom of the world." The stakes are "gargantuan," "titan." The effort, even when it fails, is to "save . . . lives, make them more ambitious, more moral, more tormented, more audacious, more ready for love, more ready for war, for charity and for invention." The task is to "explain America," if not to educate, reform, even save it (99). "A future to life," Mailer proclaims, "depends on creating forms of an intensity which will capture the complexity of modern experience and dignify it, illumine—if you will—its danger" (311).

This is the great moral and rhetorical purpose of writing for Mailer. The writer is a "physician" fighting a war against America's "plague" and "cancer," a "noble physician," "noble at least in his ideal, for he is certain that there is a strange disease before him, an unknown illness, a phenomenon which partakes of mystery, nausea, and horror; if the nausea gives him pause and the horror fear, still the mystery summons, he is a physician, he must try to explore the mystery" (5). The war which Mailer's writing records is a war against the wordless. If he is compelled by the extraverbal, by mystery, he is challenged to battle by the antiverbal.

Mailer sees Capote and the *New Yorker* as part of the genteel tradition which has failed the mystery, and though he grants that Capote's writing, worked out as it is in such a small and confined critical space, is "superb" in his own way, his comments on *In Cold Blood* imply his objection to Capote's style: "Edith Wharton

[has] reappeared as Truman Capote, even more of a jewel, even stingier." *In Cold Blood* is a "watered down" novel of manners, an example of cultural realism diminished to mere "documentary." In his "aristocratic narrative sensibility" Capote has "never seen the task of defining the country as one for him—it was finally most unamusing as a task" (99).

We can easily see what's underneath this criticism. As Mailer says of himself in the introduction to *Cannibals and Christians*, he has "yet to submit to the prescription laid down by the great physician Dr. James Joyce—'silence, exile, and cunning.'" The patient in Mailer's view is simply "too gregarious" for such a prescription (5). Mailer is anything but silent. He is explicit, self-dramatizing, polemical, continually featuring himself in the act of battling against what he proclaims to be the evils of the country. Capote is clearly Joycean, by nature silent, cunning—detached as narrator, dramatizing rather than arguing or railing. Interestingly, in this context Mailer would have to make the same charge against Wolfe. Though Wolfe is not at all subtle stylistically, though he has great energy and nerve, though he also celebrates the plebeian tradition over and against the genteel, he is simply too detached for Mailer's taste. He does not declare himself, engage in the high argument.

But from the broader perspective I've been trying to develop in this book, Mailer's intense advocacy only clarifies a tension, a war, that is integral to the style and structure of Wolfe's and Capote's work. An explicit, first-person point of view does not equal advocacy. The question is not the degree of commitment but the kind. Wolfe and Capote may be informative where Mailer is deliberative, may recreate and inhabit the experience rather than critique it from the outside, but in the end they share and act out Mailer's concern about the dangers of the antiverbal. Mailer's defense of rhetoric in *Armies* only makes more explicit Wolfe's and Capote's similar commitment to the power and authority of language. The rhetoric of silence, we have seen, conserves even as it expands. Wolfe invests himself in language even in the act of trying to reach beyond it. Capote's silences are not a retreat but a stylistic response to the inexplicable, a style which demands a style. We may critique the efficacy of these rhetorical responses—Wolfe's, Capote's, Mailer's—but we need to see all three as responses to the same central problem, the problem of inexplicability, efforts similar in kind to order and shape a complex experience.

The real political issues do not have to do with "left conservatism" or the war in Vietnam. The real act of deliberation does not lie in direct argument and the statement of a political position. Because the conflict here is between words and wordlessness, style itself is the crucial political act. "Democracy," Mailer says, "flowers with style; without it, there is a rot of wet weeds." We value the memory of Roosevelt and Kennedy not because of their specific policies but because "they offered high style to the poor. And that is worth more than a housing project. That is the war against poverty" (*Cannibals* 52). All three writers we have been exploring offer a high style as a war against the poverty of the American spirit. It is a style which challenges equally the bourgeois and the nihilistic, the complacent and the out of control. "Style is character" for all three (*Cannibals* 210). It suggests the heroism of the writer in the act of trying to comprehend enormity.

V

In light of all that I've said about *Of a Fire on the Moon* and *Armies of the Night*, *The Executioner's Song* is a disturbing, a puzzling book. On a first reading it seems radically different in style and approach from the first two books, perhaps even a repudiation of that self-dramatizing, polemical voice, the baroque, hyperbolic style. The Ruminator becomes the Recorder: the language is flat, stark, bare. Though the narrator is omniscient he does not intervene. The style is documentary, mere recitation of fact, transcription of materials.

Two passages chosen at random suggest the flavor, or the absence of flavor, in this prose:

> Gary was invited to dinner that night at Sterling Baker's house. He made quite an impression on Sterling's wife, Ruth Ann, by playing with the baby for a long while. Since he liked the music on the radio, he bounced the baby in time to Country-and-Western. Johnny Cash, it came out in conversation, was his all-time favorite. One time he got

out of jail and spent an entire day listening to nothing but Johnny Cash records. (32)

At V.J. Motors, there was a 6 cylinder '66 Mustang that seemed to be pretty clean. The tires were fair, the body was good. Spencer thought it was a reasonable proposition. The car sat on the lot for $795, but the dealer said he would move it at five and a half for Spence. It beat walking. (62)

The language continues in this vein for over a thousand pages, rarely varying in tone or emphasis, and this is the key to its effect. With a minumum of organization and intervention, Mailer takes us from one point in Gilmore's life up to the end, relentlessly recording all the trivia, all the meaningless details of his experience, reproducing the texture of his life without making it meaningful or giving it a literary shape. It's as if he has set a camera down in the middle of this event, in the tradition of Warhol and cinéma vérité, and simply recorded all that passed the camera's eye. The obvious flatness of the language mirrors the randomness of detail. Few nouns are modified. Most sentences are simple and of the same length. Mailer tells rather than shows, engaging in summary rather than dramatization. After the first hundred pages or so, the reader is ground down by the droning plainness of the recitation. Where are the nuances, the complexities, the metaphorical stunts of *Fire* and *Armies*? Where is the intensely self-reflexive, philosophizing narrator, the narrator filtering all experience through his own peculiar and passionate sensibility?

Even the voice of the recorder disappears over the course of the book, giving way to the voices of the people Mailer is describing. "The Gilmore business would probably be the only thing he'd worked on that they might still write about fifty years from now," Mailer says of Earl Dorius, the prosecutor for the Gilmore case. "After Gilmore, sob, sob, my life will be downhill" (679). This is not Mailer's own language; the Mailer of *Armies* does not write, "Sob, sob." This is Earl's language, the language of a small-time Mormon lawyer about to prosecute his most important case. "Nicole walked into this funky one-story jail," Mailer writes, "went down a couple of short corridors, passed a bunch of inmates who looked like beer bums, then a couple of dudes who whistled as she went by, twirled their mustaches, showed a bicep, generally acted like the cat's ass" (298). "Funky," "dudes," "beer bums," "cat's ass" are clearly Nicole's terms, too banal, too adolescent, too middle-class, to be Mailer's own, except perhaps in mimicry. Certainly it is Mailer who puts these phrases into a series of parallel predicates, organizing what in Nicole's own statement would undoubtedly be a set of fragments or short sentences. But except for this elementary syntactic ordering, Mailer has chosen virtually to reproduce the substance of Nicole's answer to an interviewer's question.

Throughout the book Mailer's language carries more than traces of the interview transcripts which are the foundation of his research. He is omniscient only in the sense that he does not put quotations around his slight rephrasings of Nicole's or Vern's or Gilmore's own statements. Each separate paragraph—and they are separate from the beginning, surrounded with blank space—carries the sense of text: each is a transcription of some documented response from the participants in the drama.

In fact, Mailer's language often resembles the raw, fragmentary language of note-taking. Farrell "went through the questions," Mailer writes, "and emphasized the possible follow-throughs. Did his best to psyche them up" (754–55). As in hundreds of similar phrases in *Song*, Mailer doesn't transform the fragment into a complete sentence, as if he is merely typing up his notes about the event rather than synthesizing or reworking them:

> Gibbs was in there, chain-smoking. Schiller's first impression was of a small, slimy, ratty, jailhouse guy. Red squinty eyes. He had a receding hairline, a Fu Manchu goatee, a little dingbat mustache. Bad teeth. Pale as a ghost. A guy who would stick a shiv under your armpit. Farrell liked him even less. He looked like a poor old weasel sitting there. The total stamp of jail was on the man. (755)

The short sentences, the listing of facts, the even briefer fragments, all give the impression of Mailer quickly noting what he sees rather than assimilating and judging. The prose seems undigested. In a sense, perhaps, we are closer here even than in *Armies* or *Fire* to the dramatization of process, the story of the effort to recover the event. The raw, unedited data of research is prior to the self-dramatization of the ruminator. The transcription of voices without stylistic melding presents data for the ruminator to analyze. It's as if Mailer, rather than writing a book, chooses to present us with the material he would have to work from in writing a book.

This apparent refusal to synthesize or select or arbitrate culminates in long stretches of virtual collage where Mailer simply pastes together clippings from the papers and fragments from Gilmore's letters or interviews. One whole chapter in the second half of the book, for example, consists of, in this order, an open letter from Gilmore published in the *Provo Herald*, pornographic selections from Gilmore's prison notebook, and a short article in the *Salt Lake Tribune* about Gilmore's relationship with a young pen pal in Massachusetts (784–89), each with only a minimum of intervening transition from Mailer. The next chapter consists of three letters from Nicole to Gilmore and one of Gilmore's replies, here without any intervening commentary. Other long sections in the center of the book are nothing more than verbatim sections of Gilmore's interrogation or his interviews with Stanger or Boaz or Schiller. As Diane Johnson observes in the *New York Review of Books*, the style of the narrative is often "pure tape recorder," a "spin-off from the mini cassette" (3).

In short, in *The Executioner's Song* Mailer employs the same authorial silence he attacks in Capote. Though he takes Capote and others to task for failing to order the complexities of the American experience, for resorting to strategies of "silence, exile, and cunning," though he claims it is the responsibility of the writer to dramatize his own efforts to shape and interpret the inexplicable, in *The Executioner's Song* he seems to have failed at ordering himself. Comparisons with Capote's *In Cold Blood* are inevitable, of course, and the reviewers have been quick to make them. But the important point of similarity is not their similar themes but their similar technique, not their focus on murder but their way of focusing. Both Mailer and Capote approach the act of murder with an omniscient detachment, never intervening in the narrative directly.

Yet the comparison also distorts. Capote shapes and selects, seeking out metaphor and fact, featuring irony and symbol through the careful orchestration of plot and characterization. Mailer's comparison of *In Cold Blood* to a "jewel" is useful: the book is finely wrought, tightly structured, each sentence crafted, each image meaningful and evocative. But *The Executioner's Song*, both because of its length and because of the absolute flatness of its prose, is far from jewel-like. Mailer tries to contain more than Capote, it is true; he tries to take more on. But at the same, each image and sentence in the book is lost in a mass of fact and surface and recorded statement. On a first reading no one theme or pattern of metaphor stands out. Detail is flatly metonymic, pointing nowhere, not as in Capote richly symbolic, evoking theme. If any of the texts we have examined in this book justifies Zavarzadeh's notion of "zero-degree interpretation," it is *The Executioner's Song*. The result is what we can only call tedium. If in Capote we are drawn into the narrative, excited and intrigued by the suspension of detail, in *The Executioner's Song* we are flattened, bored, frustrated by the endless accumulation of surface and fact.

But on a second reading stylistic traces of Mailer's earlier voice begin to emerge, examples of a language that could only come from Mailer himself as author behind the silent poses, and these serve to direct the flow and meaning of the text, rendering its very flatness and superficiality figurative. A voice emerges which gives us the key to reading the voice of the recorder as ironic, a way of disclosing Mailer's sense that the Gilmore story is fundamentally meaningless, representative of a void.

The very disparity between the flatness of *The Executioner's Song* and the richness of the earlier books is enough to suggest that form here is significant. Mailer is too self-conscious about the implications of style, too committed to the value and authority of language, not to be employing authorial silence for specific rhetorical ends. As he puts it in *Armies*, "one discloses what one knows about a subject by the cutting edge of the style employed" (170). Form in Mailer is always the shape of a content, an index to theme. Voice is argument, and it changes as the subject changes, disclosing Mailer's response to his subject in every subtle shift and movement.

We discover the key in *The Executioner's Song* at precisely those moments where the language becomes denser, more metaphorical, more rhythmically controlled: "It was time to recognize, Brenda decided gloomily, that when you had Gary around, there were questions for which you would not get answers. The snow kept coming down. Out on the roads, the universe would be just one big white field" (48). Against the bare outline of Mailer's otherwise toneless reporting, the evocation of landscape stands out in sharp relief. The first sentence is obviously a paraphrase of part of Brenda's own testimony, but the focus on the snow and the whiteness of the fields is novelistic, an effort to create atmosphere through what Wolfe would call status detail. It is metaphorical: the universe is like a white field. Moreover, because the comparison is juxtaposed with Brenda's observation about Gilmore's inexplicability, it carries over into a comment about Gilmore himself. What Mailer suggests is the absence of distinctions, the inability to discriminate among details in a wide field of detail. The white field seems a metaphor of vastness and meaninglessness, and it is aligned here with what Brenda suspects is the impossibility of understanding Gilmore's inner self.

Mailer evokes a similar landscape and atmosphere when he describes the effort of one of the detectives in the case to understand Gilmore's tape-recorded confession:

> The prison [where Gilmore was interviewed] sat on the edge of the desert in a flat field of cinders midway between the ramp that came off the freeway and the one that went up to it. The sound of traffic was loud, therefore. Since a spur of railroad track also went by, boxcars rumbled through the interview. When Nielsen tried listening to the tape recorder in his office, the sound of traffic on a hot summer evening was the clearest statement he could hear. (285)

It is novelistic simply to describe a landscape: we do not ordinarily detail a setting in recounting events; the emphasis in conversation or testimony is on the facts and the essentials of plot. Moreover, the detail of the traffic noises is not typical of the scene. It seems peripheral at first, even incongruous. The language here is denser as well, the diction more evocative: "flat field of cinders," "spur of railroad track," "boxcars rumbled through the interview." To put it simply, these are not the kinds of observations we would expect the detective himself to make, except perhaps in passing, and this is clearly not the kind of precise, focused language we would expect him to use in recalling the detail. The voice we hear is Mailer's, and the image we see him evoking is again the image of flatness, starkness, emptiness, again in conjunction with Gilmore's motives and inner self. The tape recording of Gilmore's confession is drowned out by the random, droning noises of freeway traffic— and freeways, not incidentally, are one of Mailer's favorite images of the American cancer.

Toward the end of the book there is still another landscape of blankness. In describing the thoughts of one of Schiller's secretaries on the eve of the execution, Mailer writes: "She had always thought 'existential' was an odd word, but it now was so bleak and cold outside, just a little bit of eternal snow on the ground, and she felt as if no one had ever gone out of this motel with these Xerox machines, and the typewriters" (879–80). The fact of pattern suggests significance. Repetition signals meaning, and by this point the importance of snow, of bleakness, of emptiness is unmistakable. This is not "Lucinda's" language. This is Mailer taking her testimony and investing it with "existential" meaning. What he wants us to see is the pointlessness, the dreariness of the Gilmore story. He wants us to key on the repetition and generation of page after page of Gilmore's written analysis and testimony, volumes of Schiller's often tedious interviewing. Xeroxing is here an image of flatness, drabness, pointlessness. Words blur on the page. Snow obliterates all distinctions of building and rock.

We begin to notice a similar emphasis in the description of interiors. The mobile home where Gilmore's mother lives is narrow and depressing: "everything was a shade of brown. One poverty after another. Even the icebox was brown. It was that shade of gloom which would not lift. The color clay. Nothing would grow" (495). The psychiatric ward where Nicole is committed "depressed the hell out of her—like she was condemned to live in a visiting room forever" (633). In their concreteness and conciseness, descriptions like these signal the presence of the author behind the masks. Bessie and Nicole do not use setting to evoke mood and theme; Mailer does. His emphasis is on "poverty," on absence, on the breakdown of meaning, the possibilities for communicating. Perhaps we attend to these passages more than to the flat recitations surrounding them because we know from Mailer's other writing that he despairs of the drab architecture and plastic aesthetic taking over the American landscape. We know that as author he must view interiors like these with distaste and revulsion. In any event, the effect here is to create an atmosphere of despair and at the same time boredom, lifelessness.

The pattern culminates in Mailer's account of Farrell and Schiller's effort to draw Gary out in their interviews:

> Farrell and Schiller agreed that the trick was to get Gary to talk truly about the murders. Something always happened then. Gilmore's readiness to comment on himself disappeared. His account fell into the same narrative style every hustler and psychopath would give you of the most boring, or of the most extraordinary evening—we did this and then, man, like we did that. Episodic and unstressed. Resolute refusal, thought Farrell, to attach value to any detail. Life is a department store. Lift what you can. (798)

This may be Farrell's own observation; he is after all a journalist, a literate man. But in the context of the book as a whole the comparison of Gilmore's language—and his personality—to life in a department store is telling, a clear indication of how Mailer means us to understand Gilmore's experience. The passage has authority because it continues a pattern, and the pattern stresses Gilmore's fundamental lack of depth, the superficiality of his experience and the experience of all those around him. The "resolute refusal . . . to attach value to any detail" is precisely the idea figured by the snow field or the flat field of cinders. What Gilmore's life illustrates is the fundamental mundaneness of part of America. As Gilmore's mother puts it, "it was like a void had entered the house" when her son returned from reform school (467).

From this perspective other masses of detail begin to take shape.

Throughout all his many interviews and sessions of self-analysis, Gilmore is never able adequately to explain why he committed the murders. He is never able to explain himself. Over and over again in response to questions he tells his interviewers: "hey . . . I don't know. I don't have a reason" (288). He blanks whenever he tries to explain just what was going on in his head at the moment of the murders, turning instead to peripheral details and external circumstance. "What I do," he says, "is the absence of thought" (800), void of content, motive. Psychiatrists and journalists search for underlying motivation—problems at home, latent homosexuality, rebellion against false standards of decency represented by Mormonism—but in the end Gilmore resists such characterizations. He acts not out of hatred or repression but out of some motiveless malignancy. "He's giving it off the top," Schiller begins to suspect over the course of their interviews. Underneath there is no deeper reality. Schiller asks: "how did you feel when you got your sentence? was it fair?" Gilmore replies: "I probably felt less than anyone in the courtroom." "How would you describe your personality?" Schiller asks next: "Slightly less than bland." As he struggles to understand Gilmore's personality and feeling, Schiller comes to realize that the murders express a deep and even terrifying void. The transcripts of their interviews contain a great deal of "blank space," silences occurring at just those junctures where there ought to be revelation. Over and over again the tapes and the transcripts come back from prison "empty of content" (801).

Part of the problem is that Gilmore is a man of poses and masks. Underlying each separate motif in Gilmore's written replies, Farrell discovers twenty-seven different voices: the tough guy, the con man, the poet, the mystic, the sexual deviate, and so on. With journalists or psychiatrists Gilmore will develop elaborate psychological protocols, but with a cellmate he will brag about the true senselessness of what he did:

> "I am telling them that the killings were unreal. That I saw everything through a veil of water." Now they could hear the drunk moaning again. "'It was like I was in a movie,' I say to them, 'and I couldn't stop the movie.'"

"Is that how it came down?" asked Gibbs.

"Shit, no," said Gilmore. "I walked in on Benny Bushness and I said to that fat son of a bitch, 'Your money, son, and your life.'" (357)

Gilmore's joking about the murders is no more authentic than his more sober reflections. Rather, for Gilmore there seems to be no governing depth or motivating inner self. "By God," Farrell asks himself near the end, "was Gary like Harry Truman, mediocrity enlarged by history?" (828). The answer, Mailer implies, is yes.

Gilmore's dependence on written texts is important in this light. In the end he has written hundreds of letters to Nicole and others, pages and pages of autobiographical manuscript. After the first suicide attempt he writes ten pages a day—"the total had to be well over a thousand pages." "Gilmore was writing about everything" (709). And his interviews and testimony are all on paper, transcribed from conversation and tape recordings. Eventually Farrell and Schiller conduct their interviews entirely on paper, submitting written questions which Gilmore then answers in writing. The story of Gilmore's execution represents the ironic triumph of language, all the reality of the case absorbed into words, assimilated into writing. Pieces of these many documents compose Mailer's long stretches of often pure collage, and his paraphrased omniscience reflects similar documents, though indirectly.

Ultimately Gilmore becomes more interested in the aesthetics and interrelationships of language than in the truth the language purports to communicate. He listens carefully to his own voice on tape, worries about the style of his written answers, revises, adds, deletes. In prison he becomes both writer and literary critic of his own writing. His concern is with image, with how the press will interpret his statements, how he will appear to the public. "I don't know it till I see it in writing," he says at one point, and later: "I'm a literal man" (644, 804).

Textuality figures superficiality. These are just words, just black marks on a page, words generating more words, pages duplicating themselves. Paper is thin and flat; the components of the collage are mere surface. Gilmore has emptied himself into the two-dimensionality of the page, flattened himself out into mere language. As texts proliferate, as page after page falls into line, we begin to see that language does not signify. It is the antithesis of depth:

> I got into a search for Truth real heavily at one time. I was looking for a truth that was very rigid, unbending, a single straight line that excluded everything but itself. A simple Truth, plain, unadorned. I was never quite satisfied—I found many truths though. Courage is a Truth. Overcoming fear is a Truth. It would be too simple to say that God is truth. God is that and much, much more. I found these Truths, and others. (345)

This is one of the few letters where Gilmore does more than repeat pornographic phrases or complain about prison conditions. On the surface it seems to be expressing some "truth" or philosophy. But only on the surface. Surely the Mailer who attacks the vacuousness of the New Left or the bland technologese of Johnson's rhetoric must see in Gilmore's trite clichés and adolescent, capital letter philosophizing another example of the debasement of language. These are Hallmark card platitudes, the wisdom of the mobile home court, and even they give way in most of these letters to unimaginative obscenity.

Of course, all of this has implications for the way in which the press generates rather than discovers the reality of the Gilmore experience. The press participates in the perpetuation of language for its own sake, divorced from any real correspondence in the world of fact. Its interest is in "really good quotes," usable "dramatic material" (544). The reporters pursue "scenarios" and "approaches" rather than reality. Ironically, in their search for some underlying truth in Gilmore's life or character, they entirely miss the point that the heart of things here is a void. Unable to find an antihero or romantic misfit, they manufacture one in their copy. The talent of the press, Schiller observes, is "turning one thing into another" (876).

There *is* an underlying, unavoidable reality in the end. Underneath or behind the press coverage is the fact of death, and the terror of death. This is the ultimate fascination of Gilmore's story.

The news of Gilmore's coming execution "lived in the air of the courtroom" on the day of sentencing. "It was as if there had been one kind of existence in the room, and now there was another: a man was going to be executed. It was real but it was not comprehensible. The man was standing there" (447). Death is a "terror" we like "to keep away back to its far-off place" (936), perhaps because it levels all language, exposes the superficiality of words. Words "wear down" in the days before Gilmore's execution. On the day itself, as prison officials prepare Gilmore for the chair, you could hear the warden going "blah, blah, blah" but no one listens. As the moment approaches there is silence:

> Three or four men in red coats came up and put the hood on Gilmore's head. Nothing was said after that.

> Absolutely nothing said. (985)

Temporality undermines rhetoric, to echo the title of Paul de Man's famous essay. Imagination takes flight from the void. Schiller, who up to now has indulged in journalistic hyperbole and romanticizing, chooses to recount the event in flat, detached, objective prose, describing rather than hyping. The song of the executioner is perhaps a whistling in the dark, language trying to cover up a darkness, a void.

But the disparity between words and death only underscores Mailer's emphasis throughout *The Executioner's Song* on the superficiality of Gilmore's experience. Death is only the logical extension of the void that exists in Gilmore. In a black irony at the end of the book, Mailer dwells in detail on Gilmore's autopsy. The brain is removed, the heart; the body is left behind, empty and lifeless, a metaphor for the emptiness Gilmore always carried with him.

From this perspective, Mailer's authorial silence, his grouping together of texts in an unmediated collage, makes stylistic sense. In its resemblance to raw data, to unedited note taking, Mailer's prose in *The Executioner's Song* suggests his inability to assimilate or sort out the experience. Emptiness and meaninglessness are a kind of inexplicability, not sublime as in *Fire* or *Armies* but just as problematic stylistically. The center is wordless. The zero-degree quality of the language mirrors Mailer's inability on one level to find an explanation, an overarching order.

Similarly, the proliferation of texts without interpretation or arbitration on Mailer's part dramatizes the fact that none is definitive, all equally suspect. Length and textuality are figurative in this sense, an ironic index to the complexity of the experience. As Schiller says, "if I can't find the story, then nobody can find it. But if nobody can, then it has to be a good story" (586). As in Capote, the rhetoric of silence dramatizes a rhetorical failure which indirectly magnifies the presence of what it cannot articulate. The very failure to encompass the experience suggests its magnitude. Schiller's editor comments, "I'd be afraid to cut a word," even though the manuscript is 10,000 words over the contracted length (1032). Where to cut? After the execution is over and the writing is done, Schiller still dreams of the project, and in all those dreams he is a "writer without hands" (1043). The material is vast, chaotic, bizarre, resisting easy formulation. Flatness, an attempt at accuracy, even at the expense of selection and conciseness, is the only stylistic alternative.

The dull, police-report voice of Mailer's actual description of the murders carries with it an undertone of shock: "Gilmore brought the automatic to Jensen's head. 'This one is for me,' he said, and fired" (224). That's it. The violence and terror and meaninglessness of the act are telescoped into two matter-of-fact sentences which do not explain themselves. There is nothing to say, nothing that can be said, and that starkness, that refusal to be hyperbolic, conveys the violence and terror more powerfully than any long, melodramatic elaboration.

But more than that, Mailer's style in *The Executioner's Song* is meant to mirror the meaninglessness of the event. Our experience as readers of the book—tedium, frustration, the inability to discriminate—is itself figurative. The tediousness of the book is a long, sustained irony, even a parody. Mailer's flatness and refusal to interpret guarantee him against the hyperbole of the press. The voice of the recorder, which contains all the exaggerations and distortions of the major news networks and news magazines, is meant as parody of the effort to generate rather than discover the drama. But even more important than that is Mailer's parody of the pointlessness and vacuousness of Gilmore's voided, empty life—and the voided, empty, drab, unimaginative, life of the Mormon middle class he grows up in. At first glance it may seem that Mailer would identify with Gilmore as psychic outlaw, a rebel against psychological constraint and sublimation. But Gilmore's language, and Mailer's, gives them away. Form for Mailer is always a response to the nature of the material, changing depending on the subject. In *The Executioner's Song* the subject is vacuum, and the language is dangerously, but appropriately vacuous itself.

Thus Mailer is still fighting the war that is form, despite the initial indications that he has given up or entrenched himself. In the broad ironies of the structure of this text, he vouchsafes himself against the meaninglessness he is imitating. He tropes meaninglessness, thus making it meaningful. As a strategy this is risky. It requires much greater participation from us as readers than before in Mailer's work. Gone is the self-dramatizing narrator who makes it clear how we should understand and war against the apocalypse. As Mailer explained to William F. Buckley in a "Firing Line Interview":

What I discovered at a certain point—and I think this is really the core of it—is I thought, I can write a book that will really make people think in a way they haven't quite thought before. This material made me begin to look at ten or 20 serious questions in an altogether new fashion, and it made me humble in that I just didn't know the answers. I mean, I've had the habit for years of feeling that I could dominate any question pretty quickly—it's been my vanity. And it was an exceptional experience to spend all these months and find that gently but inevitably, I was finding myself in more profound—not confusion—but doubt about my ability to answer, to give definitive answers to these questions. But what I had instead is that I was collecting materials that I would think about for the rest of my life. In other words, I was getting new experience. I thought it might be very nice for once just to write a book which doesn't have answers, but poses delicate questions with a great deal of evidence and a great deal of material and let people argue over it. I feel there are any number of areas in this book where there are people who have better answers to give than I have. (Hellman 60)

Mailer's tone has changed. He has been "humbled," beaten back perhaps in the battle against unmeaning. Yet he makes clear that authorial silence is a rhetorical gesture designed to elicit the reader's participation. It is not a capitulation to nihilism but a demand for reading. Throughout his work Mailer has struggled to elicit reaction and participation—through insult and challenge, through obscentity, through self-parody and confession, through stylistic density and metaphorical baroqueness. Authorial silence is another weapon in this arsenal.

Indeed, to the extent that we accept Mailer's invitation to participate in the making of meaning, we ourselves move inside the text. The threshold Mailer is trying to penetrate is that which exists between writer and reader, text and reader. Silence heals that breach. As readers we begin to fight the war ourselves. We begin to create order.

4

The Cat in the Shimmer

I

In an essay on the motives and methods of her writing, Joan Didion develops a peculiar image to define the purpose of her prose:

> There used to be an illustration in every elementary psychology book showing a cat drawn by a patient in varying stages of schizophrenia. This cat had a shimmer around it. You could see the molecular structure breaking down at the very edges of the cat: the cat became the background and the background the cat, everything interacting, exchanging ions. People on hallucinogens describe the same perception of objects. I'm not a schizophrenic, nor do I take hallucinogens, but certain images do shimmer for me. Look hard enough, and you can't miss the shimmer. It's there. You can't think too much about these pictures that shimmer. You just lie low and let them develop. You stay quiet. You don't talk to many people and you keep your nervous system from shorting out and you try to locate the cat in the shimmer, the grammar in the picture. ("Why I Write" 6–7)

The characteristic strategies of Didion's prose style are part of her effort to locate the cat in the shimmer of American experience. She lies low in her writing, looks hard at America to discover the pictures that shimmer, the images that resonate. She stays quiet, allowing the pictures in her mind to develop their own shapes and grammars. The grammar of her writing is the grammar of radical particularity. The rhetoric of her prose is the rhetoric of concreteness and implication, symbol and gap, process and struggle.

Two of Didion's most representative essays—"On Going Home" and "On Morality" (*Slouching towards Bethlehem* 164–68, 157–63)—illustrate the several dimensions of this style.

The central strategy of Didion's prose is what I will call the rhetoric of particularity. By temperament, she claims, she is incapable of thinking "in abstracts" or traveling in the "world of ideas." Her mind by its nature "veers inexorably back to the specific, the tangible," to "the physical fact" ("Why I Write" 5). Her habitual gesture as a stylist is to isolate the ironic or symbolic or evocative image and then reflect on its possible significance.

"On Going Home" is a virtual collage of such images: "the pretty young girl on crystal" who takes off her clothes in a San Francisco bar; memorabilia from an old dresser drawer emptied onto a bed; a trip to the family graveyard, where vandals have overturned the monuments. The essay is a list of details, a juxtaposing of scenes. And the scenes shimmer, evoke meanings. In the evening after her daughter's first birthday, Didion kneels beside the crib and touches her face through the slats:

> She is an open and trusting child, unprepared for and unaccustomed to the ambushes of family life, and perhaps it is just as well that I can offer her little of that life. I would like to give her more. I would like to promise her that she will grow up with a sense of her cousins and of rivers and of her great-grandmother's teacups, would like to pledge her a picnic on a river with fried chicken and her hair uncombed, would like to give her *home* for her birthday, but we live differently now and I can promise her nothing like that. I give her a xylophone and a sundress from Madeira, and promise to tell her a funny story.

This is the conclusion of the essay. But rather than close with generalizations about the collapse of the American family, Didion dramatizes herself at a particular place and time. She conjures the values of "home" with what Wolfe would call the "status details" of teacups and river picnics. The concreteness of the scene carries the burden of meaning, just as earlier the image of the topless dancer implied the rootlessness of the young and the vandalized graveyard suggested the loss of tradition. In Booth's terms, Didion "shows" rather than "tells" her longing and her regret in the scene by the crib.

In "On Morality" Didion begins by confessing that she is simply unable to think "in some abstract way" about what can be considered moral in America, the assignment she was given by *The American Scholar*. Her mind, she says, anticipating "Why I Write," "veers inflexibly toward the particular"—to the story, for example, of a talc miner who stayed on a desert highway in the middle of the night guarding the corpse of an accident victim. "You can't just leave a body on the highway," the man's wife explains. "It's immoral." For Didion the story resonates. It is a cat that shimmers. The question of "whether or not a corpse is torn apart by coyotes," whether "we will try to retrieve our casualties, try not to abandon our dead," gives rise to a complex meditation on ethical conduct. The story embodies the theme.

The second grounding particular of the essay is the story of a diver searching the underground pools of a desert watering hole for the bodies of two drowned men:

> They have been diving for ten days but have found no bottom to the caves, no bodies and no trace of them, only the black 90 degree water going down and down and down, and a single translucent fish, not classified. The story tonight is that one of the divers has been hauled up incoherent, out of his head, shouting—until they got him out of there so that the widow could not hear—about water that got hotter instead of cooler as he went down, about light flickering through the water, about magma, about underground nuclear testing.

The image of the diver's madness and the flickering of light in the contaminated water—isolated, set apart on the page, featured—is representative of the images that ground all of Didion's essays: her vision in *The White Album* of the great dynamos of a California dam still churning after Armageddon, "transmitting power and releasing water to a world where no one is" (201); her memory of an autumn afternoon her sophomore year at Berkeley, "lying on a leather couch in a fraternity . . . reading a book by Lionel Trilling and listening to a middle-aged man pick out on a piano in need of tuning the melodic line to 'Blue Room'" (*White Album* 205). In *Salvador* the crystallizing images are anecdotes and stories from the war. The story of a government commandante who thought a group of American nuns and priests were French because the word used to describe them was always "Franciscan"—this, for Didion, is "one of those occasional windows that open onto the heart of El Salvador" (49). The story of the spokesman for a native crafts exhibit who explained that the "traditional way" of obtaining wicker for making native furniture has always been to import it from Guatemala—this is a particularly "instructive moment" (73). The diver's vision in "On Morality" is clearly "instructive," a "window" to the interior of the experience Didion wants to describe. It carries for her the suggestion of danger, of imminent catastrophe, implies what we will see is her sense of America's impending apocalypse. "Here are some particulars," the key transitional phrase in the beginning of the essay, is an index to Didion's method throughout her work. She is a framer of pictures, an arranger of images.

Closely related to the rhetoric of particularity in Didion's prose—in fact, ultimately a function of it—is the rhetoric of gaps, the withholding of interpretation and commentary at every level of language. There are gaps, for example, between sentences in "On Going Home," a deliberate omission of transitional words and phrases. After discussing the apparent irrelevance of home for the postwar generation, Didion immediately moves, within the same paragraph, without explicit transition, to the description of the topless dancer contest. There is the small space following the end of the previous sentence, then: "A few weeks ago in a San Franscisco bar I saw a pretty young girl on crystal take off her clothes and dance for the cash prize in an 'amateur-topless' contest." The juxtaposition is abrupt and dislocating. It is only after a momentary regrouping, a brief comparing of what came before and after the break, that we realize how the topless dancer is meant to illustrate Didion's comment about the irrelevancy of home.

Similar gaps take place between paragraphs. "We get along very well," Didion says at the end of the third paragraph, "veterans of a guerrilla war we never understood." A paragraph break follows, and then two sentences, "Days pass. I see no one." There is structural coherence here. The paragraphs follow one another chronologically, recording separate vignettes of experience in their order of occurrence. But because Didion deliberately leaves out the connections, we are required to engage in a split-second more of active interpretation.

In this way "On Going Home" recalls "Slouching towards Bethlehem," where Didion uses more obvious sections of blank space to separate deliberately fragmentary and unrelated scenes, portraits, dialogues, and stories, creating a verbal collage. She uses a similar technique later in "The White Album," the title essay of her second volume of essays, as well as in "The Morning after the Sixties," "On the Road," and a number of other pieces in this collection. As she explains in "Why I Write," white space is also the structuring principle of her second novel, *Play It As It Lays*. She wanted to write a book, she says, "in which anything that happened would happen off the page, a 'white' book to which the reader would have to bring his or her own bad dreams" (7). Even sentence rhythm in "On Going Home" suggests fragmentation, as in the asyndeton of "Days pass. I see no one." Didion's sentences are unadorned and straightforward, connected by blank space rather than conjunctions. Parallel structure indicates parallel relationships, but for the most part there is no hierarchy or subordination in these series.

There are similar gaps following Didion's short interpretive statements. The difference between Didion's "home" in Los Angeles and her original "home" in Sacramento is a "vital although troublesome distinction." Why? Didion doesn't elaborate. Instead she immediately turns to a listing of concrete details. When Didion says that she and her mother "get along very well, veterans of a guerrilla war we never understood," she does not elaborate. We can gather the meaning, and do. It is clear from the context of details that precede the statement. But Didion does not explicate the statement. It is commentary, it is interpretation, but it demands interpretation itself. It is stark, terse.

Most importantly, Didion's radical particularity in itself involves a kind of gap or silence. Rather than explain her feelings about the disjointedness of her own past, Didion inventories childhood treasures: "A bathing suit I wore the summer I was seventeen. A letter of rejection from *The Nation*, an aerial photograph of the site for a shopping center my father did not build in 1954." Why didn't her father build the shopping center? And what does that fact mean? Why include it? Didion doesn't say. She lets the fact resonate. Rather than tell us that her family is uncommunicative and out of touch, she provides a one sentence dramatization: "We miss each other's points, have another drink, and regard the fire." Each scene is preceded or concluded with interpretive statements, but because these interpretive statements are short and suggestive rather than elaborated, the scenes bear most of the burden of significance. We must read them.

Sometimes the details are metonymic, triggering associations in the reader's mind which lead to a fuller impression of the scene. On this level they involve a gap or silence, since one phrase or image on the page carries with it a larger unspoken context, a context we recreate from the written clue. In other cases the images are synecdochic, symbols of some larger meaning. Didion's mention of snakes in the graveyard clearly evokes the notion of evil and danger. Here, too, like Capote, Didion means more than she says. What she says is the scene itself; what she means is what the scene points to, signifies.

There is more connecting commentary in "On Morality." Didion precedes and follows each central image with more extensive interpretation and analysis. But here, too, the images shimmer in the blank space surrounding the words. The shimmer is silent. The story of the diver ends with a paragraph break; the next paragraph begins with a comment on the "tone" of the event but then moves on to more concrete listings. Didion doesn't interpret the image. She "lies low and lets it develop." She "stays quiet." She doesn't, in a sense, "think too much about the picture that shimmers." She simply describes it, features it on the page. "Every now and then I imagine I hear a rattlesnake," she says, "but my husband says that it is a faucet, a paper rustling, the wind. Then he stands by a window, and plays a flashlight over the dry wash outside." The paragraph ends and Didion goes on to philosophical considerations. The image of the flashlight playing over the dry wash is left to echo in our minds, a symbol perhaps of light illuminating darkness, perhaps of the futile effort to fend off the evil hiding in the desert night.

The third characteristic strategy of Didion's prose is the rhetoric of process. The commentary Didion offers is highly tentative, grounded in the moment of the writing, a function of her effort at that place and time to think through a problem in language. "I am home for my daughter's first birthday," Didion says, then: "By 'home' I do not mean the house in Los Angeles where my husband and I and baby live, but the place where my family is, in the Central Valley of California." Rather than revise the first sentence to include a more precise definition of "home," Didion makes an initial statement and then records her modification, her qualification of the statement in a subsequent sentence. "Marriage is the classic betrayal," she says, then, after a paragraph break: "Or perhaps it is not any more." Rather than synthesizing the two interpretations of marriage offered in these two paragraphs, Didion records both, apparently in the order of their occurrence. The thinking and the writing seem simultaneous. We are left with the impression that Didion is exploring the theme *in* writing, transcribing her reflections at the instant they occur, allowing the various versions of her thought to stand side by side rather than cancelling the abandoned interpretations or resolving the ambiguities in fixed, balanced sentences. "I *am* home," she says [italics mine], here and now, in the moment of the writing.

The parentheses, repeated predicates, multiple conjunctions, and cumulative modifications of her sentences reflect this sense of spontaneity. "I would like to give her more," Didion says of her daughter, then goes on to refine, rethink, qualify the statement: "I would like to promise her that . . . would like to pledge her a picnic on a river . . . would like to give her *home* for her birthday . . ." The appositive is her characteristic modifier, a redefining noun phrase placed after the main clause as a kind of unpacking of the initial generalization: "When we talk about sale-leasebacks and right-of-way condemnations we are talking in code about the things we like best, the yellow fields and the cottonwoods and the rivers rising and falling and the mountain roads closing when the heavy snow comes in." The movement of her sentences is cumulative, from statement to subsequent modification in free modifiers, a movement which parallels the way the mind actually seems to work in the act of thinking, first fixing on an idea, then discovering its qualifiers and extensions. Often Didion resorts as well to simple addition, as in this representative sentence from "John Wayne: A Love Song": "It was called *The Sons of Katie Elder*, and it was a Western, and after the three-month delay they had finally shot the exteriors up in Durango, and now they were in the waning days of interior shooting at Estudio Churubsco outside Mexico City, and the sun was hot and the air was clear and it was lunchtime" (*Bethlehem* 33). Simple coordination suggests the unpremeditated movement of the mind as it discovers the sometimes arbitrary details of immediate experience.

In "On Morality" Didion dramatizes her thinking in still more obvious ways. "As it happens," she begins, "I am in Death Valley, in a room at the Enterprise Motel and Trailer Park, and it is July, and it is hot." In the rest of the paragraph she goes on to explain how she is struggling to write about the subject at hand but repeatedly finds herself returning to the immediate particulars of her own experience. Rather than present a finished and deductive analysis on the question of morality, Didion tells us the story of her thinking about the question, in all its stubborn concreteness and nonlinearity. "Particularly out here tonight, in this country so ominous and terrible that to live in it is to live with antimatter, it is difficult to believe that 'the good' is a knowable quantity." This is not an abstract disquisition remote from us as readers. The ideas seem to unfold in the moment of composition. They are a function of a particular place and a particular time, grounded in the real moment of the desert night. As the essay proceeds Didion seems actually to carry on a dialogue both with the reader and with herself as she reflects with us on what she has written in each previous paragraph: "You are quite possibly impatient with me by now: I am talking, you want to say, about a 'morality' so primitive that it scarcely deserves the name," or, after describing the possibility of rattlesnakes in the drywash: "What does it mean? It means nothing manageable."

"I write entirely to find out what I'm thinking, what I'm looking at, what I see and what it means," Didion says in "Why I Write" (6). Writing for her is a means of discovery and problem-solving, a way of reflecting on what the pictures in her mind might mean. She begins writing with the problem, not the solution. "I want to explain to you, and in the process perhaps to myself, why I no longer live in New York," she writes in "Goodbye to All That" (*Bethlehem* 227). This is the characteristic gesture, a metadiscursive reference to us as readers which calls our attention to the fact of the writing as an act in itself taking place before our eyes. "I had better tell you where I am and why," she begins "In the Islands": "I am sitting in a high-ceilinged room in the Royal Hawaiian Hotel in Honolulu watching the long translucent curtains billow in the trade wind and trying to put my life back together" (*White Album* 133). And in the present moment of these acts of discovery and probing, Didion's conclusions can only be tentative and qualified, marked by "perhaps," "maybe," "I don't know," acknowledgments of fear and anxiety, self-contradiction. Occasionally, too, the writing yields insight, and always in the now of the composition: "As I write this I realize," she stops to add in *Salvador*, or "When I think now of that day in Gotera I remember . . ." (30, 43).

Taken together these three strategies constitute a form remarkably similar to that of the romantic lyric in early nineteenth century England. Didion's essays contain all the elements of the lyric as Robert Langbaum defines it in the *Poetry of Experience*: a specified place and time, an individualized speaker, a dramatized process of thought. The experience she describes in "On Going Home" or "On Morality," in Langbaum's terms, is "dramatized as an event which we must accept as having taken place, rather than formulated as an idea with which we must agree or disagree." It is "located," an "occurrence," "something which happens to someone at a particular time and in a particular place." Her essays do not illustrate a "ready-made truth" but rather "tell the story of the making of the truth" (41–64).

More to the point, the signature techniques of Didion's writing represent the fulfillment and the attenuation of the essay as a form. I mean "essay" here as opposed to strict journalism. As Wolfe notes, there is a fundamental difference between the work of an investigative journalist, a reporter who does extensive research and legwork in the field, and that of the "literary gentleman with a seat in the grandstands," the more "genteel" familiar essayist who refects on his own experience or on the events and situations readily observable around him ("New Journalism" 43). Strictly defined, journalism requires research and investigative reportage; the "essay" does not. Didion, of course, has done her share of journalism—"Some Dreamers of the Golden Dream," *Salvador*—but I would argue that her most important and representative work falls into the category of the essay. Her characteristic strategy is to reflect on contemporary life from the standpoint of her own experience or to engage in autobiographical narrative which ultimately leads to commentary on the social problems of the time. She sees her subjects in terms of the self. Even her reportage has the quality of reflective/exploratory writing. She does not attempt the "saturation reporting" that distinguishes the New Journalism, and her presentation of fact is almost always a point of departure for personal reflection and meditation.

Seen from this perspective Didion's writing is the latest moment in the development of the essay from the "leçons morale" of the Renaissance to the personal reflections of Montaigne to the loosely autobiographical ramblings of Hazlitt and Lamb. Montaigne's first essays are attempts to bring together helpful passages in his reading and preserve useful lessons from the ancients, very much in the tradition of Plutarch or Erasmus. The goal of all Renaissance leçons, as William Bryan and Ronald Crane explain, was to "collect and make readily accessible the views and discoveries of the ancients on all questions relating to the conduct of life" (xii). At first, leçons were in fact loose collages consisting of an impersonal, unoriginal grouping of maxims and examples. The subjects were all general and commonplace. But Montaigne's temperament soon led him to blend these adages together with examples from his own experience and then to develop these personal applications into narratives and reflections which assumed an independent interest of their own. As he developed the form of the essay, maxims and examples gradually became subordinated to personal reflection.

According to Leslie Fiedler, this is the central movement in the history of the essay since Montaigne: a movement away from the topical or general and toward the particular and personal. From Montaigne "in a direct line descend all essayists who remain essentially autobiographers, all explorers of the self, who seek clues to that self directly in their own lives and the trivial details of their daily routines" (2). In Fiedler's view the formal and didactic writing of the periodical essayists of the eighteenth century is an aberration, a deviation in the natural evolution of the form. In the eighteenth century, "the speaking voice, the conversational tone, is lost everywhere beneath the long, carefully balanced periods and the embroidery of classical allusions" (2).

I would argue that the familiar essay of Hazlitt is a return to the central tradition of the form. Crane and Bryan note that the essay of the early nineteenth century is no longer confined to town and society. The emphasis is on the individual's personal experience as well as on contemporary history, just as the emphasis in romantic poetry is on the expression of the self in the time and place of lyric inspiration. Here, of course, is the connection between the form of the romantic lyric as Langbaum describes it and the form of the essay.

But my point is not to develop a full and detailed history of the essay but rather to suggest in a general way that along with E. B. White and George Orwell in the twentieth century, Didion fulfills the tradition of Montaigne: she is tentative and exploratory; she sees her personal experience as an index to larger issues and social problems. But she also extends the form. Bits of experience replace the adages of the leçon. Where the gaps or white space in the leçons represent the absence of personal applications or concrete examples, the gaps in her collages represent the omission of commentary, the absence of reconciling generalities and commonplaces. The commentary that does exist is terse, highly qualified, often an explanation of why any definitive intepretation is impossible in the context of contemporary experience. Montaigne blends maxims together and applies them to his own experience, finally making the general subordinate to the particular; in Didion the general comes close to disappearing entirely. In Montaigne autobiography serves the ends of social commentary. Didion engages in useful and significant social commentary, as I will try to show, but it is important to recognize that commentary as a set of explicit interpretations is rare in her work. Didion's social criticism is a matter of style and implication, process and image—it takes place in the shimmering of the cats, the struggle enacted on the page to understand the meaning of the pictures in her mind. Montaigne grounds the generic in the personal; Didion avoids the generic almost entirely.

I have said that Didion's work is not "reportage" in the sense of investigative journalism. But we might say at the same time that the rhetoric of particularity, gap, and process represents the fulfillment in the essay form of the movement Richard Weaver describes as a shift from inference to reportage—reportage in the sense of "photographic realism," the adherence to concrete and unique detail ("Old Rhetoric" 172). Her work is an important hybrid of the essay and journalism: her journalism is essay-like; her essays are journalistic.

Finally, the three characteristic strategies of Didion's writing bring together in the smaller space of the essay the major strategies we have explored in Wolfe, Capote, and Mailer. Like Wolfe, Didion relies on the evocativeness of the status detail. Like Capote, she employs authorial silence, maintains a controlled reticence. Like Mailer, she dramatizes herself in the act of thinking through an important problem in language. Where Wolfe and Mailer are expansive and far-flung, Didion, like Capote, remains cautious, reserved, enclosed; yet at the same time she shares Wolfe's and Mailer's range of interests and subjects, their concern with the whole spectrum of American culture. She combines Mailer's metadiscursive and I-centered rhetoric with Capote's detachment, Wolfe's instinct for the ironic conversational phrase or representative anecdote with Capote's restraint and precision. In her condensed and careful essays, the techniques of the New Journalism reach their highest level of polish and refinement.

II

In a very real sense all three of these strategies are the result of Didion's failure to word an experience which she repeatedly defines as apocalyptic, paralyzing, and finally inexplicable.

There are hints of her rhetorical dilemma in "On Going Home" and "On Morality." Didion's deep concern is the loss of "home" in the "fragmentation" of America after World War II, a general undermining of order and cohesiveness at all levels of society. She fears the "white dead dawn" of nuclear destruction as well as the contaminations of underground nuclear testing. She senses "some sinister hysteria in the air" of the desert, emblematic of a building tension in society. The inexplicable is also private and personal. It lies in the "nameless anxiety" that colors her relationship to her family, their "deliberately oblique ways," their poignant inability to talk with one another. It lies in the mysteries of time and age and personal loss characteristic of all families.

A clearer articulation of Didion's sense of the inexplicable, the chaotic, the overwhelming, comes in the preface to *Slouching towards Bethlehem*, where she expresses her fear, in the words of Yeats' "Second Coming," that the "center is not holding" and that some "rough beast" is slouching towards America. It comes, too, in the opening paragraph of the title essay of the volume:

> It was a country of bankruptcy notices and public-auction announcements and commonplace reports of casual killings and misplaced children and abandoned homes and vandals who misspelled even the four-letter words they scrawled. It was a country in which families routinely disappeared, trailing bad checks and repossession papers. Adolescents drifted from city to torn city, sloughing off both the past and the future as snakes shed their skins, children who were never taught and would never now learn the games that had held the society together. People were missing. Children were missing. Parents were missing. Those left behind filed desultory missing-persons reports, then moved on themselves. (84)

Didion repeatedly figures the apocalypse in terms of family: missing children, missing parents, the loss of order and the debasement of the social languages and codes transmitted by families. For her the catastrophe is a matter of "social atomization" taking place in a "social vacuum," of children "who grew up cut loose from the web of cousins and great-aunts and family doctors and lifelong neighbors who had traditionally suggested and enforced the society's values" (*Bethlehem* 122–23).

"Casual killings" are another figure of apocalypse for Didion, as for Capote. In *The White Album* she represents her dread in the archetypal bike-movie image of gang-rape and unprovoked, mindless beatings: "To imagine the audience for whom [such images] are tailored, maybe you need to have sat in a lot of drive-ins yourself, to have gone to school with boys who majored in shop and worked in gas-stations and later held them up" (101). She is disturbed by a similar kind of violence in El Salvador, a place "without solid ground," with "no reliable depth," a place where racial hatred is "the ineffable element at the heart of [a] particular darkness," a place of "impenetrable interiors" where the "ineffable" fact of extreme violence is only expressible in the astonishing numbers of the daily body counts (13, 74, 49, 61).

Didion also represents her sense of the inexplicable in the apocalyptic landscapes of Southern California, particularly in the season of the Santa Ana, when the Pacific turns "ominously glossy," the peacocks "scream," and the heat becomes "surreal." During one particular Santa Ana, Didion's only neighbor "would not come out of her house for days, and there were no lights at night, and her husband roamed the place with a machete" (*Bethlehem* 218). The fires and earthquakes and droughts of Los Angeles are the metaphors of dread: "The City burning is Los Angeles's deepest image of itself." Its weather "is the weather of catastrophe, of apocalypse." It "shows us how close to the edge we are" (*Bethlehem* 220–21). Nothing is stable, nothing permanent. All is under the threat of "grave solar dislocation" (*White Album* 209).

In short, America for Didion, as seen from the perspective of Southern California, is a nation "characterized by venality and doubt and paralyzing ambiguities," a nation where "dread is so acute" for even the most casual citizen that conventional social values no longer can apply. The "apprehension" is "unspeakable" (*Bethlehem* 30, 63, 14). There is "peril," too, "unspeakable peril, in the everyday" (*Play It As It Lays* 100). For Didion growing up brings the recognition of evil and the possibility of randomness. As she matured, Didion says in "On Self-Respect," she "lost the conviction that lights would always turn green for me, the pleasant certainty that those rather passive virtues which had won me approval as a child automatically guaranteed me not only Phi Beta Kappa keys but happiness, honor, and the love of a good man" (*Bethlehem* 143).

In "The White Album" Didion clearly defines the rhetorical problem of trying to order this chaos in words, trying to represent the intensity and proportions of this vision in the form of the essay. Here she establishes that her style as a writer is a direct response to the atomization of her world. The images and stories that make up most of the essay are all representative of what in *Salvador* she calls the "familiar ineffable" (96): a young mother who left her five-year-old daughter alone on Interstate 5; the Ferguson brother murders and the Manson trial; a recording session for the Doors, the prophets of "apocalyptic sex." The character of the time, the sense of "imminent destruction," is reflected in the seediness of what she calls her "senseless killing neighborhood" (15). "A demented and seductive vortical tension was building in the community. The jitters were setting in." Dogs barked every night and "the moon was always full." The "sense that it was possible to go 'too far,' and that many people were doing it" is so pervasive on the night of August 9, 1969, that no one is surprised when the early garbled reports of the Manson murders start coming over the phone. Yet at the heart of it all there is an "awesome and impenetrable mystery," Didion says, something "unspeakable" (43).

Didion's version of the inexplicable, then, is much closer to Mailer's than to Wolfe's or Capote's. She does not share Wolfe's enthusiasm for the intensities of the subculture, nor Capote's fascination with mystery. There are moments, as we will see, when she defends the existence of certain positive mysteries over and against the incursions of mechanism and bureaucracy, but for the most part Didion's vision of America is more somber and despairing and fearful than any we have seen. Like Mailer she feels the center flying apart, but unlike Mailer she does not confront the whirlwind and try to harness its power or move its direction through sheer force of will.

As she goes on to explain in "The White Album," Didion's personal response to this unspeakableness is an attack of "vertigo and nausea" which renders her unable to cope with her life except at the most basic levels (15). Her response stylistically is the abandoning of conventional technique as irrelevant and beside the point. In the apocalyptic world of the sixties Didion finds that she has "mislaid" the "script" for understanding events. "I was meant to know the plot, but all I knew was what I saw: flash pictures in variable sequence, images with no 'meaning' beyond their temporary arrangement, not a movie but a cutting-room experience" (13). In a world where the conventional connections no longer obtain, the form of discourse is reduced to particularity—"flash pictures"—and gaps—the blank space transitions of the "cutting-room." Discourse becomes a collage of images, not a "narrative," not, that is, an orderly presentation of judgments. The experience which discourse must articulate is "rather more electrical than ethical," and thus language can no longer sustain unifying interpretations.

"In this light," Didion says later in the essay, "all narrative was sentimental," all connections "equally meaningful, and equally senseless" (44). By "narrative" here Didion seems to mean not simply plot but more a Boothian notion of narrative coherence and interpretative structure:

> During the years when I found it necessary to revise the circuitry of my mind I discovered that I was no longer interested in whether the woman on the ledge outside the window on the sixteenth floor jumped or did not jump, or in why. I was interested only in the picture of her in my mind: her hair incandescent in the floodlights, her bare toes curled inward on the stone ledge. (44)

The recourse of the mind in the face of meaninglessness is to the concrete and singular detail. In the face of apocalypse the meaning of images becomes suspect and finally irrelevant; only the image itself, in all its irreducible physicality, has reliable shape.

Didion makes exactly the same gesture in "In the Islands": first she confesses the inability to make certain "connections" or to maintain "the basic notion that keeping promises matters in a world where everything I was taught seems beside the point"; then she deliberately rejects the possibility of generalized social commentary:

> I could indulge here in a little idle generalization, could lay off my own state of profound emotional shock on the larger cultural breakdown, could talk fast about convulsions in the society and alienation and anomie and maybe even assassination, but that would be just one more stylish shell game. I am not the society in microcosm. I am a thirty-four-year-old woman with long straight hair and an old bikini bathing suit and bad nerves sitting on an island in the middle of the Pacific waiting for a tidal wave that will not come. (*White Album* 135)

Unable to unify the fragments of "cultural breakdown" or provide answers to the problems of social "convulsions," Didion can rely only on the immediacy of her own experience. This is what she knows, what she can attest to. When abstraction is no longer possible, when order is no longer possible, the best we can hope for is the vividness of particular fragments. More than that, Didion's radical particularity in this passage includes her self-dramatization in the act of writing. As we saw in Mailer, when discourse is impossible—when the writer cannot claim final conclusions about the subject itself—metadiscourse results, language turning away from its inexplicable object and back onto itself. She may not be able to tell the story of America, but she can describe her effort to tell the story.

All these responses to the inexplicable have affinities with similar responses in Wolfe, Capote, and Mailer: Mailer's metadiscourse before the symbol of Apollo 11, Capote's reticence before the silencing of Perry's violence, Wolfe's attempt to use the concreteness of situation as "code" for suggesting unspoken realities. But in Didion these strategies and displacements combine to create a tighter, more personal, more highly wrought stylistic response. Didion's reaction to the wordless resembles more, on the surface at least, a retreat, a defensiveness, a sublimation.

In her later work Didion continues to link her rhetoric of par-

ticularity, gap, and process to the nature of the experience she is
forced to describe. The image in *Democracy* is of a "5.2 on the
Richter scale" wrenching the writing table in her room. The narrator of the novel is a "Joan Didion" very much like the Didion of
the nonfiction, and her task as narrator is somehow to explain the
experiences of a family shaken by earthquakes both personal and
cultural. The experience, this Joan Didion frequently complains,
"tend[s] to deny the relevance not only of personality but of narrative." The suffering and absurdity of Inez Victor's life leads the
narrator to question the capacities of language: "I began thinking
about Inez Victor and Jack Lovett at a point in my life when I
lacked certainty, lacked even that minimum level of ego which all
writers recognize as essential to the writing of novels, lacked conviction, lacked patience with the past and interest in memory;
lacked faith even in my own technique" (17). Her structural solution to this rhetorical problem is to present a series of significant
images and then to reflect with us on what they might mean, often
dramatizing her own failure to formulate an interpretation. "You
see the shards of the novel I am no longer writing," she says after
explaining the various ways she might have written the novel had
she developed more conviction, more insight: "I lost patience . . . I
lost nerve" (29–30). *Democracy* is curiously reportorial in technique; Didion takes pains to give the illusion that Inez and Jack
are contemporary figures whom she has come to know over the
course of several years and must try to interpret from the outside,
assembling all the available facts. What the reportorial structure
of the novel dramatizes is the tension between words and wordlessness, the failure of the writer to come to terms with a para-
doxical and tragic reality. For that matter, all the narrators of Didion's novels are put in the position of trying to interpret an
enigmatic, representative other: the narrator in *Play It As It Lays*
struggles to understand Maria; Grace in *A Book of Common
Prayer* undertakes the narrative in the hope of understanding the
meaning of Charlotte's experience in Central America.

This is the tension, too, at the heart of *Salvador*. Recording
ironic details in a Salvadoran shopping center, Didion suddenly
realizes that she "was no longer much interested in this kind of

irony, that this was a story that would not be illuminated by such details, that this was a story that would perhaps not be illuminated at all, that this was perhaps even less a 'story' that a true *noche obscura*" (36). She turns away from the stores and walks back to her hotel, "straight ahead, not wanting to see anything at all." The response to the opaqueness and absurdity of events, on one level, is authorial silence. There is nothing that can be said. On another level the response is to tell the story of that decision to remain silent.

Thus the rhetoric of "On Going Home" and "On Morality" can be seen as a direct reaction to a central darkness. The particularity of these pieces reflects the failure of commentary; their gaps reflect the failure of sequence and transition; their insistence on process reflects the failure of synthesis. Alone on the desert at night, Didion struggles with her realization that "morality" is a word that no longer signifies. The only reality is the desert itself and the coyotes and the underground pools and Didion's own effort as she swelters in her motel room and contemplates abstractions that do not apply. Didion's task is to express a "nameless anxiety." "There is no final solution," she says, to the fragmentation of her life, or to the fragmentation of postmodern experience (*Bethlehem* 166). Didion's obliqueness reflects her inability to word the wordless.

III

But it seems to me that even granting the urgency of the rhetorical problems facing Didion, in many ways she succeeds as a writer, perhaps more than she herself allows. What Alfred Kazin has rightly called the "graphic readability" of her style to some extent counters her own claims about the failure of language. "She has several times done a perfect piece around the fear of a nervous breakdown," Kazin notes, "and not had one." She gives a "smooth literary fervor to the constant theme of decline and fall." Indeed, in Kazin's view "the story between the lines in *Slouching Towards Bethlehem* is surely not so much 'California' as it is her ability to make us share her passionate sense of it" (190). This is the tension governing Didion's work: the ironic relationship between style and apocalypse, readability and epistemological doubt. The paradox of Didion's prose is her capacity to project apocalypse in rhetorically effective and engaging ways.

We can make a case for the rhetorical efficacy of Didion's strategies on a number of different grounds:

1. I have compared Didion's essays to Langbaum's model of the romantic lyric. Here we can note that for Langbaum the tentative and self-dramatizing form of the lyric is rhetorically persuasive precisely because it remains open-ended. Form has "validity," he argues, only when "it is dramatized as an event which we must accept as having taken place, rather than formulated as an idea with which we must agree or disagree" (43). Readers, in other words, do not respond to dogma. Rather, they identify with the efforts of an individual like themselves struggling to come to terms with experience. Walker Gibson maintains in much the same way that the appropriate tone of all discourse in the twentieth century should be "informal, a little tense and self-conscious perhaps, but genial, as between equals," and he bases this standard, interestingly, on the assumption that contemporary experience is too complex and multivarious to be encapsulated in authoritative or didactic forms of discourse (105). The rhetorical principle rests simply on what Burke calls the process of "identification" (*Rhetoric of Motives* 19ff.): to persuade means to encourage an audience to identify with us as speakers or writers. Didion creates identifications by revealing her doubts and fears and her inability to synthesize, limitations that presumably everyone in her audience shares.

2. We can also argue that Didion's strategies of particularity and process create presence, magnifying our awareness of the events she claims are beyond language. The concreteness of her prose, its sense of ongoing process, make the issues and events vivid and immediate. The idea is not then remote or abstract but present on the page, immediate and experienced, the focus of an event taking place here and now. This sense of immediacy, as the classical tradition holds, is the key to the effectiveness of any discourse. For Longinus, the capacity of imagination to bring ideas vividly "before the eyes" of the audience "not only persuades the hearer but

actually makes him its slave" (85, 89). For Bacon, the ability of the speaker to render concepts vivid and present "quickens" the mind of the audience and "many times suddenly wins the mind to a resolution" (Wallace 27, 35).

In fact, presence of this sort is the basis of an interesting figure in the rhetorical tradition, a figure we have already seen at work in Wolfe's prose: "hypotyposis" or "ocular demonstration." "A great impression is made by dwelling on a single point," Cicero says, "and also by clear explanation and almost visual presentation of events as if practically going on—which are very effective both in stating a case and in amplifying the statement" (*De Oratore* 161). What Cicero recommends is both the rhetoric of particularity and the rhetoric of process. Hypotyposis describes two levels of presence: the experience of an event rendered concretely, and the presence of the writer reflecting on the event in the now of the essay. Experience on both these levels is persuasive, moving. The argument is not thus demonstrated, perhaps not even fully presented, but implicit in the theory of presence is Piaget's notion that whatever is made "the center of our field of vision," whatever we are made most aware of, is "overestimated" in our mind and thus "overrated in importance" (Beard x). The imagery and representative anecdotes of Didion's prose, in all their detail, intensify our sense of the idea's concrete context, and as William James puts it, "what holds attention determines action" (448).

3. There are, too, the sentences themselves, perfectly crafted, clean, direct, economical, evocative. The diction is nearly flawless, each word made to count. The order and precision of the language Didion uses to describe the apocalypse is at odds with the chaos and disintegration she fears.

4. As we have seen in Capote, the rhetorical effect of gaps is to involve us, stimulate us, draw us into the text. A dramatization is more vivid and real to us because in the act of completing the gaps it creates we actually have the experience it points to. To supplement and infer what an image or a suggestion does not say, we have to put ourselves *in* the text—or, to see this another way, we have to create the text in our own consciousness. The same principle holds for the structural gaps of the collage, which encourage

us as readers to assemble the puzzle of the collage as a whole from the clues of the pieces before us.

In *Democracy* Didion is quite explicit about the dynamic of such gaps or authorial silences. As readers, she says at one point, we have surely guessed by now that Jack and Inez left Honolulu together, "most readers being rather quicker than most narratives" (160). Later she discusses "the tacit contract between writer and reader to surprise and be surprised." "The heart of narrative is a certain calculated ellipsis." The writer must know "how not to tell you what you do not yet want to know." (162)

5. Implicit here, of course, is the rhetoric of the sublime and the negative logic of figurative failure which we have been tracing in Wolfe, Capote, and Mailer. The failure to signify signifies, the breakdown of imagination implying the intensity and proportions of the unattainable object. Didion's gesture of dramatizing her failure calls attention to the nature and importance of the events off the page.

From all these perspectives Didion seems partially to heal the gaps she describes in the act of describing them. Her recourse to imagery and her telling of the effort to understand those images can be seen not as failures but as structural solutions to the problem of describing what can't be described. They are oblique strategies, requiring the cooperation of the reader. They point to or hint at or describe a part of the apocalypse. Yet rhetorically they succeed to some degree—to the extent that they involve us as readers in the discourse.

Certainly, at least, these strategies succeed in mirroring the quality of despair and failure Didion perceives in American society. "An attack of vertigo and nausea," Didion acknowledges in "The White Album," "does not now seem to me an inappropriate response to the summer of 1968" (15). The images of the time constitute an "authentically senseless chain of correspondences," yet "in the jingle-jangle morning of that summer it made as much sense as anything else did." All the questions that arose in the wake of the decade's great violence and upheaveal, questions which seemed hopeless and unanswerable in the moment itself, seem to Didion now in the moment of writing the essay "more cogent than it might at first appear" (45). That is to say, stylistic fragmentation and authorial silence or self-dramatization effectively act out the fragmentation of the experience they seek to describe. They are "appropriate," even "cogent" under the circumstances of their composition. Vertigo signifies.

But more than that, the images of Didion's prose shimmer morally. They are not mere fragments in a senseless chain, singular pictures devoid of implication. Despite Didion's own repeated protestations to the contrary, her images project meanings. Stoddard Martin has recently attacked Didion for "refusing a structure for her social analysis." He faults her for rejecting traditional social radicalism or any other kind of concrete political action and accuses her of "beating an ever further retreat into the ivory towers of style and self-contemplation." In his view Didion is part of that group of artists in this century who "renounce sympathy with the abyss and cultivate aesthetic brilliance" as an end in itself (196–98). In a far less ideological criticism, Mark Winchell faults Didion for the brevity and incompleteness of her sociological analysis in "Slouching towards Bethlehem." There are too many gaps, in effect, too many uninterpreted concrete images, and not enough connecting and reconciling commentary (51). Both Martin and Winchell seem to take Didion at her word when she proclaims her failure to interpret the apocalypse and renounces any faith in the efficacy of political solutions.

But this is finally a superficial reading of Didion's prose. It equates interpretation with explicit commentary and artistic responsibility with political advocacy:

At three-thirty that afternoon Max, Tom, and Sharon placed tabs under their tongues and sat down together in the living room to wait for the flash. Barbara stayed in the bedroom, smoking hash. During the next four hours a window banged once in Barbara's room, and about five-thirty some children had a fight on the street. A curtain billowed in the afternoon wind. A cat scratched a beagle in Sharon's lap. Except for the sitar music on the stereo there was no other sound or movement until seven-thirty, when Max said "Wow." (*Bethlehem* 106)

The prose is flat and stark. Didion makes no direct authorial comment. The image is one of the fragments that make up the collage

of the essay. It is followed by blank space rather than interpretation, then a new, essentially unconnected image. It is presented on
the page for our contemplation. Didion herself in both the preface
to the volume and the introduction to the title essay suggests that
the fragmentation of the collage form in her report of Haight-
Ashbury is meant to reflect the "atomization" of American society,
in which case authorial silence might be seen as an indication of a
failure of interpretation. But this is not our experience reading
Didion. In the context of the essay the image of the silent LSD trip
shimmers, resonates. It suggests the debasement of language characteristic of the hippies, their abandonment of structures and
meaning. It suggests randomness and banality. It is poignant and
sad. Although Didion explains in the preface that her authorial
"flatness" has led many readers to misunderstand her sympathies
(she was invited to appear on talk shows as a spokesperson for the
hippies) it is clear on a careful reading that her reaction to this
scene is not approval but despair, sadness, fear, anxiety. She concludes the essay with a similarly resonant image of a fire set by the
three-year-old daughter of a hippy couple: "The only people
around were Don and one of Sue Ann's macrobiotic friends and
somebody who was on his way to a commune in the Santa Lucias,
and they didn't notice Sue Ann screaming at Michael because they
were in the kitchen trying to retrieve some very good Moroccan
hash which had dropped down through a floorboard damaged in
the fire" (*Bethlehem* 128). The burned child of parents who are
trying to retrieve Moroccan hash through the floorboards is a
powerful image.The selfishness of the parents, their neglect of the
child, the implications of the fire as a symbol of destruction, the
chaos and disruption of the family, the failure of communication—all this is obvious in the scene, even though Didion has not
intervened directly. What she shows serves to tell.

There is little doubt that Didion's description in "On Going
Home" of kneeling by her daughter's crib and touching her face
through the slats is meant to convey a sense of longing, and love,
and regret. There doesn't seem to be any question that the image
of her great-aunts calling her by the wrong name, of her daughter
playing silently in the dust-motes, is meant to suggest the inevi-

table barriers of time and age, the inability of the family to communicate across generations. The commentary of Didion's featured images and scenes is not hard to gather in the context of her individual essays. When we chart and arrange her characteristic images over the course of her essays as a whole, patterns of significance and meaning become even clearer: images of fire, earthquake, destruction on the one hand, images of family, community, safety, shelter, relationship, harmony on the other.

Indeed, Didion is frequently quite explicit in articulating her values and in offering social commentary. She does not restrict herself to the implications of concreteness but often engages in direct—though invariably short-clipped—interpretations of the American scene. I want to consider her fully articulated point of view in more detail in the last section of the chapter. Here let me suggest two important features of this philosophy, this set of meanings.

The first is obvious in light of what we have already seen. Didion laments the loss of family and tradition. In her essay on the Las Vegas marriage industry, she criticizes in clear terms the "merchandising of 'niceness,' the facsimile of proper ritual, to children who do not know how else to find it, how to make the arrangements, how to do it 'right'" (*Bethlehem* 82). What mass and instant marriages represent for Didion is the debasement of "proper ritual," a distortion of the sense of time ("One Moment Please—Wedding"), the perversion of commitment. The casual relationships of the hippies in Haight-Ashbury represent a similar undermining of the concept of family. What the conventional press fails to understand, Didion maintains, is that the counterculture is not simply an adolescent rebellion against the establishment. In Haight-Ashbury, "we were seeing something important. We were seeing the desperate attempt of a handful of pathetically unequipped children to create a community in a social vacuum" (*Bethlehem* 122). Didion would like to maintain the notion of "home" in its traditional sense and pass it down to her own daughter. The Sacramento of her childhood "resembles Eden," even though her earliest memories are of it vanishing, changing, becoming compromised. While she is aware of its self-delusions and hypocrisies, she writes movingly of a "Sacramento lost," a society of rivers and farmland and close-knit families. Such longings do not lead to political solutions in Martin's sense, but neither do they constitute a retreat to the realm of pure style: Didion interprets, takes sides. Her values are not veiled, even if they are not quite retrievable.

Secondly, Didion is not reticent in her attacks on the complacency of the middle class. In "Many Mansions," Governor Reagan's official residence becomes an objective correlative for the banality of bourgeois California. Unused and unoccupied, it is neither a "white elephant" nor "a monument to the colossal ego of our former governor," but

> simply and rather astonishingly an enlarged version of a very common kind of California tract house, a monument not to colossal ego but to a weird absence of ego, a case study in the architecture of limited possibilities, insistently and malevolently "democratic," flattened out, mediocre and "open" and as devoid of privacy or personal eccentricity as the lobby area in a Ramada Inn. (*White Album* 69)

The thirty-five exterior wood windows are to be "draped," blocking out any view of the outside. The walls "resemble" local adobe but are in fact made of "the same concrete blocks, plastered and painted a rather stale yellowed cream, used in so many supermarkets." The bedrooms open out onto a nonexistent swimming pool. A wet-bar dominates the living room. "In the entire house there are only enough bookshelves for a set of the World Book and some Books of the Month, plus maybe three Royal Doulton figurines and a back file of *Connoisseur*," yet "there is $90,000 worth of other teak cabinetry, including the 'refreshment center' in the 'recreation room.'" The kitchen is designed for microwave defrosting and trashmashing, not the making of meals or the coming together of families for meals. Every detail of the huge house represents for Didion the unimaginativeness and resolute superficiality of contemporary American life, mechanized and unread.

She prefers the Victorian asymmetry of the original governor's mansion, an "extremely individual house, three stories and a cupola and the face of Columbia the Gem of the Ocean worked into the molding over every door," built in 1877 in what is now a seedy part of Sacramento. It is a building of vast stairs and varied cubbyholes. "The bedrooms are big and private and high-ceilinged and they do not open on the swimming pool and one can imagine reading in one of them, or writing a book." The bathrooms are "big and airy and they do not have bidets but they do have room for hampers, and dressing tables, and chairs on which to sit and read a story to a child in a bathtub." In the kitchen there are no trash compactors and no appliance island, but there are two pantries, and "a nice old table with a marble top for rolling out pastry and making divinity fudge and chocolate leaves" (71–72). Taking a tour of the mansion one morning, Didion discovers that the dozen or so women in her group have no idea what the marble tabletop is for, and this becomes for her an index to the loss of tradition and style: "It occurred to me that we had finally evolved a society in which knowledge of a pastry marble, like a taste for stairs and closed doors, could be construed as 'elitist,' and as I left the Governor's Mansion I felt very like the heroine of Mary McCarthy's *Birds of America*, the one who located America's moral decline in the disappearance of the first course" (72).

Here, near the conclusion of the essay, Didion's observations about "taste" subtly but unmistakably blend into "moral" commentary. More is at stake than taste in architecture. What emerges from the carefully modulated descriptions of "Many Mansions" is Didion's impatience with the tastelessness and ignorance of the middle class. Like Mailer, she sees in America's architecture the symptoms of the cancer eating away at American society. She is an "elitist" in this context: a believer in the subtleties and disciplines of style. And the styles she defends are not merely old-fashioned or quaint but ways of accommodating the real, concrete lives of people.

Her impatience, even her rage, emerge more strongly in a portrait of an evangelical preacher in "Notes toward a Dreampolitic." What disturbs her about Brother Theobald is his simplistic insistence that God has instructed him to sell his church in Los Angeles and move the congregation to Murfreesboro, Tennessee. He seems to her naïve, ignorant of history. "Other people leave towns like

Murfreesboro, and they move into them." Brother Theobald "seemed to be one of those people, so many of whom gravitate to Pentecostal sects, who move around the West and the South and the Border States forever felling trees in some interior wilderness, secret frontiersmen who walk around right in the ganglia of the fantastic electronic pulsing that is life in the United States and continue to receive information only through the most tenuous chains of rumor, hearsay, haphazard trickledown" (*White Album* 98). The group is young and white and "nominally literate," yet "they participate in the national anxieties only through a glass darkly." It's not their conservatism that bothers Didion, their eschewing of makeup and short skirts. She is disturbed by the implications of Brother Theobald's ignorance that the courthouse at Murfreesboro had been standing since the Civil War. "In the interior wilderness," Didion says, "no one is bloodied by history" (99).

From this perspective Didion's refusal to come to reconciling conclusions, the steadiness of her insistence that the center is not holding, takes on a pointed rhetorical purpose. She is not simply giving up the hope of meaning but rather attempting to bloody her readers with recent history, rouse them with images of the electronic ganglia and the national anxieties. She is not simply lamenting the decline in architecture but explaining both the function and meaning of marble pastry tops—the need for such tabletops—to the ladies in the tour group. She wants to disrupt connections for those who make connections too easily. She wants to convince her readers of apocalypse.

My point is not to dismiss Didion's claims about her failure as a writer, about the necessary failure of any writer in contemporary America, but rather to put these claims in perspective. *The White Album* begins with Didion's anxieties about the limits of language and the failure of connection, but the rest of the volume qualifies those fears. In essay after essay she finds images that shimmer and connect. She establishes meanings. The introductory essay, after all, is an account of a past despair written in the past tense, and it implies Didion's effort to move beyond her original paralysis. As she puts it at the end of one particular scene: "At that time I believed that my basic affective controls were no longer intact, but now I present this to you as a more cogent question than it might at first appear, a kind of koan of the period" (46). The very writing of the essay implies that Didion has moved from "at that time" to the cogency of the narrative "now."

This is not to say that her shimmering images offer definitive solutions or interpretations. They are tentative moments in the process of Didion's thinking about an "unspeakable" reality (*White Album* 73). The gaps, I think, are real gaps. But the language that comes after each gap records the effort to find meaning. The dramatization of the mind in the act of thought imposes in the end a narrative line. What we have in Didion's books—taken now as volumes, as single works with different movements—is the story of a mind seeking significance, and that story, it seems to me, in its concreteness and urgency, is as compelling as any individual story Didion might tell along the way.

IV

Let me take this argument one step further. I have suggested that despite her legitimate claims for the inadequacy of language, Didion's language to some extent succeeds, both in representation and in interpretation. It succeeds in projecting a sense of what cannot be described, and it manages to offer analysis of those images, an intepretation of their moral significance. There is a further dimension to this paradox. Always qualifying and compromising Didion's despair about the inexplicable is a great faith in the power of words for good or ill. She is profoundly metadiscursive in her writing, everywhere concerned not simply with the experiences she is trying to describe but with the language of those experiences—with the jargon, the rhetoric, the diction of individuals and groups and how that language reflects a point of view. In her essays she is, more than anything else, a rhetorical critic. And this is the source of her social and political commentary, as well as the key to the social and political significance of her style.

Perhaps Didion's most frequent gesture is to put an important word or phrase in quotation marks: "home," "morality." What she hears in an interview or notices in a situation is the sound and texture and connotations of the words. In "Slouching towards Bethlehem," for example, her interpretation of the Haight-Ashbury experience turns on the implications of the hippies' clichéd vocabulary. "They are less in rebellion against the society," Didion argues, "than ignorant of it, able only to feed back certain of its most publicized self doubts, *Vietnam, Saran-Wrap, diet pills, the Bomb*." Their tragedy is that they cannot read, cannot speak in consecutive sentences, have not been taught the disciplines of language. In their view words are the property of the establishment, of "typeheads," the corrupted tools of the power structure. But without a belief in words, "their only proficient vocabulary is in the society's platitudes":

> As it happens I am still committed to the idea that the ability to think for one's self depends upon one's mastery of the language, and I am not optimistic about children who will settle for saying, to indicate that their mother and father do not live together, that they come from a "broken home." They are sixteen, fifteen, fourteen years old, younger all the time, an army of children waiting to be given the words. (*Bethlehem* 123)

Didion's commitments are not unclear or hesitant. Despite her conviction that words are finally inadequate for encompassing the intensity of American experience, she is committed to the power of language as a maker of meaning and culture. This is what drives her persistent rhetorical criticism. Over and over again in "Slouching" she dramatizes situations in which language degenerates into cliché or silence. My mother was "kind of a bummer," a young girl says when Didion asks her why she ran away. "It was really weird" (91). Or there are scenes like the afternoon trip in Barbara's room, when the curtain billows and the cat scratches and no one says anything from three-thirty to seven-thirty, except near the end when Max says "Wow" (106). When the children settle for "Wow" rather than mastery of words, when they accept the pat phrases rather than probing the complexities of real experience, the gyre begins to widen. Language is not a symptom but the cause: the children are in rebellion because they are ignorant of what sentences can teach them.

In *The White Album* Didion turns her hard and skeptical gaze on the jargon of Huey Newton and the Black Panthers. During their interview in the Alameda County Jail, Huey "lectured almost without pause," "running the words together because he had said them so many times before, about 'the American capitalistic-materialistic system' and 'so-called free enterprise' and 'the fight for the liberation of black people through the world.'" Didion puts these phrases in quotation marks because they seem to her devoid of real content. Throughout the speechifying she "kept wishing he would talk about himself, hoping to break through the wall of rhetoric"—rhetoric here meaning formulaic tag phrases, the easy generalizations—"but he seemed to be one of those auto-didacts for whom all things specific and personal present themselves as mine fields to be avoided even at the cost of coherence, for whom safety lies in generalization" (29–30). Didion cannot look past the language to the ideas behind it. There are no ideas behind it. The surface features of the words are the site of the drama, the place to locate the true meaning of the Black Panther movement. The central opposition is between the safety, and dishonesty, of generalization and the "specific and personal." As in "Slouching towards Bethlehem," generalizations are not to be trusted.

A similar opposition, and a similar preoccupation with language, underlie the social satire of "Bureaucrats," a report on the state Operations Center which controls "The 42-Mile Loop" of Los Angeles's most traveled section of freeway. On the one hand there are the favored phrases of the California Department of Transportation for describing their project to regulate freeway traffic: "demonstration system," "pilot project," "incident," and "verified incident." On the other hand there is the reality of the freeway itself as experienced by the real people who drive on it: an "incident" in real terms is "the heart attack on the San Diego, the jackknifed truck on the Harbor, the Camaro just now tearing out the Cyclone fence on the Santa Monica" (*White Album* 80). For Didion the obscure jargon of the Operations Center is an index to "bureaucratic terrorism." Her attack is not just on the project itself, which futilely tries to restrict the inside lanes of the freeway for car pools. More, it is an attack on the failure of a "mechanized" bureaucracy to appreciate the nearly "mystical" experience of actually driving on the Loop. "To understand what was going on," Didion says, "it is perhaps necessary to have participated in the freeway experience, which is the only secular communion Los Angeles has." Actually to experience the freeway is to let "the mind go clean," let the "rhythm" of lane changes and acceleration "take over." The bureaucrats of the Operations center, "professionally grounded in the diction of 'planning,'" are incapable of understanding this, incapable of "considering the freeway as regional mystery" (83–84). Their language, because it generalizes and obscures, because it ties up untidy actualities, prevents them from understanding the reality they are supposed to govern.

Perhaps the most devastating and systematic of Didion's rhetorical critiques takes place in her essay on the women's movement. Again she sees the issue almost entirely in terms of its language. The creation of a revolutionary "class," she says—as always placing key words between quotation marks—was the "idea" of the women's movement. The "movement" objects to women being "discriminated against" and "stereotyped" in the "woman's role." One theorist explains that "the birth of children too often means the dissolution of romance, the loss of freedom, the abandonment of ideals to economics." What Didion finds offensive and even immoral about such rhetoric is its generality, which inevitably reduces recalcitrant experience to labels which turn out not to be true for any individual case. What is left out of such grand and panoramic expressions is "all one's apprehension of what it is like to be a woman, the irreconcilable difference of it" (*White Album* 114–15).

Particularly significant in this analysis is Didion's identification with the values of "fiction," which represents for her the "irreducible ambiguities" of life. She describes herself as "committed mainly to the exploration of moral distinctions and ambiguities," as opposed to the discovery of absolutes, and thus finally "hostile to ideology." From this perspective, the instant "leap from the personal to the political" is a kind of bad faith, a "coarsening of the moral imagination" (112–13). The rhetoric of idealism—any idealism, in the women's movement or any other movement—is built on words like "always" and "everyone," "many" and "all": "During the fashion for shoes with pointed toes, she, like 'many women,' had her toes amputated"; "Should she work she was paid 'three to ten times less' than an (always) unqualified man holding the same job." To read the literature of feminism is to "recognize instantly a certain dolorous phantasm, an imagined Everywoman with whom the authors seemed to identify all too entirely." There is no necessary connection between these feminist abstractions and "the actual condition of being a woman" (114–15). The phrases are "half-truths," qualified and contradicted and compromised in myriad interesting ways by the stubborn untypicality of any individual's experience.

Underlying all these critiques—and they are representative of many other rhetorical analyses in Didion's work—are two fundamental assumptions. The first is an Orwellian belief in language as an index to morality and politics. Didion tells us in "The White Album" that she "reread all of George Orwell on the Royal Hawaiian Beach" (113). She takes the title of "Why I Write" from Orwell's essay of that title (5). In *Democracy* she makes her narrator a visiting writer at Berkeley lecturing on the thesis that "the way a writer constructed a sentence reflected the way that writer thought," and the first author on her list of featured writers for the course is Orwell. The narrator wants her students there to "consider the political implications of both the reliance on and the distrust of abstract words" (71–72), the obvious subtext being Orwell's famous "Politics and the English Language." I would argue that "Politics and the English Language" is the subtext of all of Didion's work. Her deepest interest is in the "similarities" between "style" and "ideas of democracy" (*Democracy* 71). Like Orwell, she believes in the inextricable relationship between words and ideas, believes, therefore that words can corrupt ideas, that the truth or falsity of ideas is directly reflected in the truth or falsity of the language used to express them. As the narrator of *A Book of Common Prayer* puts it, "the consciousness of a human organism is carried in its grammar. Or the unconsciousness of the human organism" (238). Style is not mere surface. "The arrangement of words matters," Didion argues in "Why I Write. "To shift the structure of a sentence alters the meaning of that sentence, as definitely and inflexibly as the position of a camera alters the meaning of the object photographed." Indeed, grammar has "infinite power" (179).

The second assumption is an Orwellian belief in the morality of the particular. Abstractions are immoral because they are too easy and because they cover up. The particular requires discipline, a mastery of complexity, a sympathy for fact, a capacity for layered and nuanced interpretation, for tentativeness, openendedness, honesty. The people Didion admires refuse abstractness and insist on individuality. Georgia O'Keefe is "simply hard, a straight shooter, a woman clean of received wisdom and open to what she sees"—and a woman, Didion notes earlier, who embodies the notion that "style is character," that "every word chosen or rejected, every brush stroke laid or not laid down," reveals who the artist fundamentally is (*White Album* 127). Being clean of received wisdom is the highest virtue for Didion. Out of all the people she describes in *Salvador*, she praises only two, an Irish and an American nun, not only because they illustrate the idea of "grace under pressure" but because they are not "much given to solutions, to abstracts: their lives [are] grounded in the specific" (47). They do not rehearse ideologies or act out of political persuasion.

In "The Morning after the Sixties," Didion puts these values in an explicitly political and moral context. Her generation, she says, is "distrustful of political highs," convinced "that the heart of darkness lay not in some error of social organization but in man's own blood." Social action seems to her "just one more way of escaping the personal, of masking for a while that dread of the meaningless which was man's fate." There is a tinge of world-weary fatalism in such statements, which Didion recognizes, but there is also, at a deeper level, a stubborn unwillingness to deny the "morally ambiguous" nature of the times. "If I could believe that going to a barricade would affect man's fate in the slightest I would go to that barricade," but "it would be less than honest to say that I expect to happen upon such a happy ending" (*White Album* 206–8). This is not an expression of resignation or a withdrawal from responsible action in the world; still less is it a product of what happens to be Didion's own temperament. Rather it is apolitical and moral philosophy rooted in a skepticism towards abstractions.

"On Morality," of course, is Didion's most important statement of a moral philosophy. "I want to be quite obstinate," she says there, "about insisting that we have no way of knowing what is 'right' and what is 'wrong,' what is 'good' and what 'evil'" (*Bethlehem* 164). Morality is finally just a word which can be used to justify any number of political actions and public policy decisions, however "facile" and "self-indulgent" or even "factitious." Morality as a word or abstraction is the tool of "the fashionable madmen," the echoing term in the "thin whine of hysteria heard in the land." This is why Didion insists on defining morality for herself in pragmatic and even primitive ways as a basic adherence to the social code of "keeping our promises" and maintaining our "primary loyalities" to each other. It is on the level of particular individual relationships and particular individual promises that we can make claims to "know" what to do. Didion uses "cautionary tales" and "graphic litanies" to illustrate what she thinks is moral: the talc miner guarding the corpse from the coyotes versus the members of the Donner-Reed party, who violated the "one vestigial taboo" against eating one's "own blood kin." But I don't think Didion is espousing a "wagon-train morality" so much as refusing to engage in the high public discourse of moralizing. What's significant about her tales is that they are tales, stories that travel by night, not theories. To insist that "the good" is not "a knowable quantity"—that it is a mystery, inexplicable—is to insist on the radical irreducibility of things.

There is, in other words, another dimension to the idea of the inexplicable in Didion. On the one hand there is the apocalypse of collapsing families and disintegrating social order. But on the other there is the fundamental inexplicability of life itself in all its radical complexity and depth and nuances, an inexplicability which for better or worse cannot and should not be reduced to simple phrases. The "unspeakable mysteries" of the everyday must finally be engaged "only personally" (*White Album* 208).

The obvious implications of this moral and rhetorical criticism for Didion's own rhetoric are most powerfully developed in *Salvador*, in my view her most successful piece of writing, both as rhetorical criticism and as rhetorical performance. From the beginning Didion's concern is with the obfuscating generalities of political rhetoric. In the "tortured code" of the American embassy and the Salvadoran government, she notes, political executions are mere "incidents," reports of mass murders nothing more than "uncorroborated stor[ies] . . . dredged up from the files of leftist propaganda" (15, 22, 19). The magazine of El Salvador's national airline can describe the volcano crater where hundreds of bodies are left to rot as "offering excellent subjects for color photography" (19).

Didion's strategy as rhetorical critic is immediately to offer concrete images of the reality such euphemisms obscure. It is a grim deconstruction. "Incidents" result in bodies "often broken into unnatural positions, and the faces to which the bodies are attached (when they are attached) are equally unnatural, sometimes unrecognizable as human faces, obliterated by acid or beaten to a mash of misplaced ears and teeth or slashed ear to ear and invaded by insects" (16–17). In El Salvador "one learns that vultures go first for the soft tissue, for the eyes, the exposed genitalia, the open mouth." One learns that "hair deteriorates less rapidly than flesh, and that a skull surrounded by a perfect corona of hair is not an uncommon sight in the body dumps" (17). These are not exercises in sensationalism and vulgarity. The language is flat and understated, a camera eye panning over the scene; the effect is to juxtapose the words used to describe death and mutilation with the plain fact of mutilated bodies. Didion climbs to Puerta del Diablo, the mountaintop where the bodies are dumped, and what she sees there is not "a view site," not "evidence of the country's geothermal resources," but "what is left of the bodies, pecked and maggoty masses of flesh, bone, hair." Standing at the rim of the dump, "we did not speak." The sight of death "induces in the viewer a certain protective numbness," Didion notes earlier of forensic photographs. Here silence is the only appropriate response. The event exceeds commentary.

Didion's approach throughout *Salvador* is first to examine the bureaucratic rhetoric of the issue and then to deconstruct it. Over and over again she unmasks the deceptions of words—with facts, with examples, with logical and grammatical analysis. American and Salvadoran officials have "cut a linguistic deal," Didion claims. "Language as it is now used in El Salvador is the language of advertising, of persuasion," and this is part of the "place's pervasive obscenity." In an analysis remarkably similar to Orwell's attack on Stalinist rhetoric in "Politics and the English Language," Didion demonstrates how words like "improvement," "perfection," and "pacification" hide grotesque events and immoral policy decisions: the stealing of family lands, the subjugation and even extermination of whole villages (64–65).

In a single sentence she cuts through the displomatic haze in the speechifying of an Assistant Secretary of State:

> "The new Salvadoran democracy," Enders was saying five months after the election, not long after Justice of the Peace Gonzalo Alonso Garcia, the twentieth prominent Christian Democrat to be kidnapped or killed since the election, had been dragged from his house in San Cayetano Itepeque by fifteen armed men, "is doing what it is supposed to do—bringing a broad spectrum of forces and factions into a functioning democratic system." (90–91)

Roberto D'Aubuisson, the leader of the Nationalist Republican Alliance, is not "young," "immature," "impetuous," "impulsive," "impatient," or "intense," as other diplomats and officials have described him. Quoting former ambassador Robert E. White, Didion calls him, simply, bluntly, "pathological," a "killer." In a speech to the British Parliament, President Reagan calls the election of D'Aubuisson to the presidency of the Constituent Assembly "a vote for freedom" (28). Didion counters with what she sees: "the naked corpse of a man about thirty with a clean bullet-hole drilled neatly between eyes," his genitals "covered with a leafy branch" (45–46). In a country where it is difficult even to estimate the number of such corpses, phrases like "human rights" and "land reform" and "the initiation of a democratic political process" are "so remote *in situ* as to render them hallucinatory" (38–39).

More than facts and logic, Didion provides images to counter the rhetoric. She describes how it feels to sit "on a canopied porch of a restaurant near the Mexican embassy, on an evening when rain or sabotage or habit had blacked out the city," and then abruptly become aware "of two human shadows, silhouettes illuminated by the headlights and then invisible again," one sitting "behind the smoked glass windows of a Cherokee Chief parked at the curb," the other "crouched between the pumps at the Esso station next door, carrying a rifle" (25–26). She describes how it feels to sit on the porch of a parish house in the interior, chatting with the American and the Irish nun:

> The light on the porch was cool and aqueous, filtered through ferns and hibiscus, and there were old wicker rockers and a map of PARRO-QUIA SAN FRANCISCO GOTERA and a wooden table with a typewriter, a can of Planter's Mixed Nuts, copies of *Lives of the Saints: Illustrated* and *The Rules of the Secular Franciscan Order*. In the shadows beyond the table was a battered refrigerator from which, after a while, one of the priests got bottles of Pilsener beer, and we sat in the sedative half-light and drank the cold beer and talked in a desultory way about nothing in particular, about the situation, but no solutions. (46–47)

These are status details, nearly random, the genuine images of the experience, and recorded as they are, not stereotyped or made to fit a standard picture of clerical life in the interior. We feel the scene as something that happened at a particular place and time to particular living people.

Underlying this radical recourse to the particular in *Salvador* is Didion's conviction that rhetoric is the cause of the crisis of American intervention. Language is not incidental; it is not simply an index to the problem. As in "Slouching towards Bethlehem," it *is* the problem. We have been "drawn" into a futile "game" in El Salvador "both by a misapprehension of the local rhetoric and by the manipulation of our own rhetorical weaknesses." We have been baited by broad and finally meaningless words like "communism" or "Marxism"—or, on the other hand, by phrases like "broad-based coalition of moderate and center-left groups"—into intervening in a country where political labels cannot obtain in any simple way. We have let the inevitable "ambiguity about political terms" involve us in pointless efforts to "secure our own interests" without ever being sure what those interests are. And our continued and deliberate use of ambiguous labels only perpetuates the problem, further dividing words from a reality whose real tragedies do not get addressed (95–96).

More importantly, Didion is convinced that the answer to this problem of language is a new language of concreteness and particularity—that the crisis of abstractness and euphemism can be met by a rhetoric of precision, imagery, and openendedness. Before she went to El Salvador, Didion says, she "knew" all about the horror of the situation there, but she knew only "abstractly": "the specific meaning eluded me until I was actually there, at the Metropolitan Cathedral in San Salvador, one afternoon when rain sluiced down its corrugated plastic windows and puddled around the supports of the Sony and Phillips billboards near the steps" (78). This is not the El Salvador of "democratic vistas" and grand "programs"; it is a place where rain sluices and puddles, and not just around the supports of any billboard, but of Sony and Phillips billboards. If she can get us to see, to experience, Didion is implying, we, too, will know more than "abstractly." Because El Salvador is "squalid beyond anyone's power to understand it without experiencing it" (88), an authentic rhetoric must dramatize the experience of being there. Anything that might be said about the country in the abstract will continue "to fall upon the ears of [the] auditors as signals from space, unthinkable, inconceivable, dim impulses from a black hole" (102). Only through images and stories can the "auditors" begin to conceive what "the fact of being El Salvador" might mean (103–5).

This is not to suggest that Didion's concreteness in *Salvador* is unbiased, uncontaminated by prejudice and interpretation. The point, of course, is that the images shimmer morally. Didion means them to convey her own position about the events in Central America. Her recourse to the particular, however, is based on a belief that particulars, even when they are framed by bias, carry greater weight and authority than ungrounded generalities with no relation to perceived, experienced fact. The link she wants to establish is not between idea and objective "fact" but between idea and felt experience.

What *Salvador* illustrates in the end is the moral and political dimension of Didion's characteristic strategies. There is a cat in Didion's shimmering, to reverse the metaphor I began with. There is more to her prose than "mere" style and readability, certainly more than the stylish resonances of her nearly perfect sentences. Beneath the shimmer is a real cat, agile and sharp clawed. All of which is to say that for Didion style is never "mere" style. "The cat becomes the background and the background the cat": the status details that make up her scenes, the surface features of the scenes themselves, are not mere embroidery but the picture itself, the center. They are details that demand detail, concreteness that demands concreteness. As in Wolfe, Capote, and Mailer, style in Didion *is* argument.

In the first part of this chapter I proposed one model for understanding the relationship between words and wordlessness in Didion: particularity, process, and gap as necessary accommodations to the limits of language. That model holds true in *Salvador* as well. Didion's frequent allusions here to Conrad's *Heart of Darkness* are apt. Like Marlow, Didion must travel to the "heart of darkness," an ineffable center where there is only "the horror, the horror." In her effort to articulate that horror, as in all her work, she dramatizes herself in the act of telling a story that can have no ending, selecting representative images and interpreting their resonance as best she can.

But in *Salvador* we have another model as well. Here it is evident that radical concreteness can also be a way of unmasking mystifications to reveal true mystery. It is an effort to identify the immoral abstractions that to some degree are responsible for the apocalypse—the abstractions which try to cover up and simplify what must remain inexplicable. Americans who have actually been in El Salvador have been "inexorably altered by the fact of having been in a certain place at a certain time" (98). The concreteness of Didion's prose—not only in *Salvador* but in all of her nonfiction—

is meant to "alter" us by giving us the experience of "having been" somewhere, having seen and felt "a certain place at a certain time." Freed from covering euphemism and all too reconciling abstractness, unencumbered by clichés and slogans, we can then engage the underlying mystery, the true mystery, for ourselves.

Conclusion: *The World's Biggest Membrane*

"Everyone says, stay away from ants," Lewis Thomas observes in "The Tuscon Zoo." "They have no lessons for us; they are crazy little instruments, inhuman," together forming "a single animal" rather than going their separate ways as individuals. "Look out for that," everyone says. "It is a debasement" (*The Medusa and the Snail* 10).

But for Thomas there is a fundamental contradiction in using language to argue that we should be "individuals, solitary and selfish":

> This is a hard argument to make convincingly when you have to depend on language to make it. You have to print up leaflets or publish books and get them bought and sent around, you have to turn up on television and catch the attention of millions of other human beings all at once, and then you have to say to all of them, all at once, all collected and paying attention: be solitary; do not depend on each other. You can't do this and keep a straight face. (10)

This is not the place to consider the styles and themes of Thomas' prose, although in many ways they fit the argument I have been making in this book. Thomas' essays are not in the tradition of the New Journalism. He is a scientist, writing about the implications of science for contemporary culture, and he adopts as his form not reportage but the reflective and exploratory forms of the familiar essay. Yet it seems to me that Thomas' notion here—that the fact of language in itself contradicts claims of disorder and disunity, that language as a system of structures and interrelationships by its nature is a unifying and socializing force—this notion gives us a useful way of reviewing the tensions and paradoxes that we have seen are implicit in the specific styles and forms of contemporary American nonfiction.

The persistent theme of Thomas' essays is that the human community should aspire to the organic interrelationships, the harmony, the selfless cooperation everywhere evident in nature: in anthills, in the social behavior of wasps and bees, in the intricate structures of the cell, in the complex ecology of the organelles and bacteria that govern the processes of the body. In a lovely image at the end of *The Lives of a Cell* Thomas imagines the entire earth as a gigantic living cell, "organized, self-contained," "full of information, marvelously skilled in handling the sun." It is a huge "membrane" catching and storing energy, "holding out against equilibrium" (145).

Thomas frequently develops the metaphor of the membrane to figure the possibilities of human community. "It takes a membrane to make sense out of disorder in biology," he says (*Lives of a Cell* 145). But ultimately for Thomas the most interesting and the most powerful membrane in nature is not found in the biochemistry of the cell or the relationships between organisms in an ecosystem. It is found in human language. "Language is, like nest-building or hive-making, the universal and biologically specific activity of human beings. We engage in it communally, compulsively, and automatically." Our ability to arrange words in syntactical order and to understand the syntax of others is innate, a built-in capacity of our minds. The instinctiveness of language thus binds and unifies us. Words are a separate living system to which we are subordinate. We work at speaking and writing all our lives, and collectively we give words meaning, but "we do not exert the least control over language, not as individuals or committees or academies or governments." Ultimately language is "alive," like an "active, motile organism," "growing, enriching itself, expanding," linking us as users of words to every other human being on the planet (*Lives of a Cell* 89–90). Each individual word is "membranous, packed with layers of different meaning," and taken together words form a system of membranous, layered meanings governing the way we live (*Lives of a Cell* 130).

It would be unfair, of course, to impose Thomas' guarded biochemical optimism on Wolfe, Capote, Mailer, and Didion. The New Journalism is not as confident as biochemistry about the possibilities of order. But the underlying argument in my analysis of the style of contemporary American nonfiction turns on much the same paradox that Thomas identifies in his defense of ants: language itself in these texts has a conserving and independent power often contradicting the claims it makes. In the subtle styles and structures of contemporary prose, words develop into a membrane, an organism, for absorbing and storing energy, releasing and conserving power. Didion's insistence on the limited concreteness of any moral stance, her scrupulous avoidance of the generic, is countered to some extent by rhetorical gaps which involve us as readers, by the affective presence of her shimmering images, by the purely formal expectations aroused and fulfilled in the structures of her collages. She proclaims our solitariness, our separateness, but she does her proclaiming in a language which creates a provisional unity in the act of reading. Despite her frontier primitivism, her prose is marked by what Perelman would call "figures of communion" (170): "I tell you this to demonstrate," "Even as I tell you this," "You see what this is," "What I want to tell you about is," (*Bethlehem* 30, 41, 66, 172, 173). Words make gestures toward communion with a reader. They imply the effort, the need to be understood, and thus a contractual relationship with the reader, which depends in turn on the common language and set of conventions reader and writer share. "And so it was," Didion says in "Some Dreamers of the Golden Dream," leading into the next section of the narrative (*Bethlehem* 13). The phrase strikes us because of its storytelling quality, its conventionality. It suggests on a basic level how language invites us to join in the fulfillment of patterns, the telling of stories.

Wolfe pursues Kesey and the astronauts, all individualists in their own way. Capote pursues the idiosyncrasies of Perry Smith and other misfits. Mailer is preoccupied with Gary Gilmore and other psychic outlaws. In a sense all the New Journalists take a stand on the side of the separate and solitary. The "right stuff" is a quality shared by heroes set apart, rejecting or transcending society. What the New Journalism celebrates is the unique, the different, the threatening, experiences and ideas beyond the pale of ordinary, communal life, set apart and therefore interesting, life on the edge. Yet the words that Wolfe, Capote, and Mailer use to develop these characters and ideas inevitably set up counter lines of force, a set of checks and balances.

All four authors I have explored in this study remain concrete in their reportage, avoiding explicit commentary or grounding their commentary in the limiting contexts of individual subjectivity. They fulfill the movement Weaver describes from "inference" to "reportage," or the shift Booth sees from "telling" to "showing." Their epistemological skepticism keeps them from indulging in the rhetorical stewardship that marks the topical discourse of an earlier age. In their concreteness, their "eye-socket" narration, their "scene-by-scene" reconstruction, their authorial silence, they engage the particular. But there are generic claims in the use of language itself. Language itself, as a membrane, as an organism, carries its own set of themes and implications.

The paradox obtains as well for the claims of wordlessness. When Wolfe, Capote, Mailer, and Didion project the antiverbal and inexplicable in a language that by its nature binds and unifies, at least in the moment of reading, they involve themselves in the ironies of form. There is an inevitable tension in claiming wordlessness in words.

In *A Rhetoric of Motives* Kenneth Burke says that "when we use symbols for things, such symbols are not merely reflections of the things symbolized, or signs for them; they are to a degree a *transcending* of the things symbolized" (192). What we have seen in Wolfe, Capote, Mailer, and Didion is the transcending of the thing symbolized, the events reported, a transcending made possible by the use of language itself. This is a fact of our reading experience. When we read *The Right Stuff* or *The Armies of the Night* or *The White Album* we do not experience despair but aesthetic ordering and transcending, the internal purposiveness of a created form adequate, at least in part, to the intensity of the world outside. Language interposes a layer of meaning between word and thing. There is a quality of distance, of difference. We do not have the experience when we read; we have an experience of reading. In *The Rhetoric of Religion* Burke notes that there is a fundamental difference between the "sun" as a heavenly body and the word "sun" written on the page. If there were no such difference, he says, we would be well advised to get as far away from the page as possible (9).

Or we can approach this paradox from the Burkean perspective of "motive." In addition to the property motive and the instinctive biological desire for possession, there is in human beings according to Burke a prior "symbolic" or "rhetorical motive," the instinct to engage in rhetorical exchange for the sake of the exchange itself (*Rhetoric of Motives* 136–37). The other motives are in fact a pretense for necessitating rhetoric, ways of creating conflict which require a rhetoric that as fundamentally rhetorical creatures we are glad to take part in. At the root of every literary work and symbolic act is the "invitation to purely formal assent." We are lovers of words. "Many purely formal patterns can readily awaken an attitude of collaborative expectancy in us" (*Rhetoric of Motives* 58). We engage in the play of formal patterns because we are by nature linguistically playful. This pure rhetorical motive, on the part of both the reader and the writer, underlies the reportage of the New Journalism as it underlies and stimulates any structured expression. In Thomas' terms, this is why the New Journalists "can't keep a straight face" when they argue for separateness in language. The irony rests on the rhetorical motive itself.

I am talking here about the innate properties of language regardless of literary or stylistic quality. My argument might apply to any act of expression, no matter how rudimentary or crude, as long as its intentions are basically coherent. Language from this perspective is an independent and suprapersonal organism surpassing any individual's intentions. But ultimately my analysis of the rhetorical consequences of style in contemporary nonfiction has rested on more than this general claim. What I have tried to suggest is that these four authors deliberately make us aware of the tensions between wordlessness and wordfulness. Their works are intensely and consistently metadiscursive, preoccupied with the problems of rhetoric. They thus call our attention to the paradoxes, preparing us to consider their reportage in light of these ironies and tensions. Furthermore, the commitment of each author, explicitly stated or repeatedly implied, is to the discipline of style and the affective power of words as shapers of experience. Each writer is first and foremost a stylist, self-conscious in his or her use of the sentence and the word. Each writer believes, as Didion puts it, that grammar has "infinite power"; that the "arrangement of words in the sentence matters."

Finally, there are the highly developed styles of the works themselves: spontaneous or carefully wrought, flamboyant or restrained, explicitly I-centered or marked by gaps, but always foregrounded, aware of themselves as language, as style. As I promised in the introduction, I have tried to analyze these styles in some detail, engaging the major texts of contemporary nonfiction in their own terms, building up a sense of nonfiction as a genre inductively, through close reading. Using both classical and contemporary rhetorical theory, I have tried to characterize the unique voice of each author: Wolfe's rhetoric of presence, Capote's rhetoric of silence, Mailer's rhetoric of self-dramatization, Didion's rhetoric of particularity. On this level I have wanted simply to catalog the various stylistic devices of contemporary nonfiction, compiling a grammar of style. But at the same time, in the process of this analysis, I have attempted to show how the translucence, the richness of the language of contemporary nonfiction accumulates its own rhetorical force over the course of individual works—how, in light of Wolfe, Capote, Mailer, and Didion's metadiscursive commentary on the challenge of language in American culture, style itself becomes a powerful argument. In this sense most of all, contemporary nonfiction takes what is the fundamental tension in any use of language and magnifies it, makes it present, transforms the prevailing irony into a deliberate claim.

I started my work in contemporary American nonfiction convinced that its central problem is the effort to express the inexplicable and that its various styles and structures are a product of that effort. My assumption was that the language must in some way fail, that there would be gaps, holes, struggling, inadequacy, because I took seriously the claims of the New Journalism for the intensity and complexity of American experience, its claims that contemporary reality exceeds language and must therefore exceed its attempts to describe it. And I think I have demonstrated that in many ways this is a useful model for understanding the tensions and struggles of contemporary prose. Each of the authors in this study posits the experience he is trying to describe as wordless; each author develops styles and strategies that must in some way circumvent the inevitable limits of language.

But as I read and reread contemporary prose, I soon discovered a countermovement in the prose, a subtext always qualifying and complicating the recognition of the inexplicable: a belief in the power of language to order and create, a belief demonstrated in the rhetorical performance of the texts themselves. Contemporary American prose is not finally about wordlessness, not about failure, but about the rhetorical power of words at a time when language is constantly being threatened. For every impulse toward silence there is a linguistic impulse, a rhetorical impulse, underneath. For every acknowledgment of failure there is a new form which gains strength and cogency from that failure. The story of contemporary American prose, the story I have tried to tell in this book, is not about the rupturing or the collapsing of the envelope of language, the death of the membrane. It is about the expansion of the membrane to accommodate new realms of experience. It is about the growth of the organism of language. This is what makes contemporary American nonfiction rich, complex, and worth close reading. This is what makes it important for American culture. From this perspective the various rhetorical strategies we have identified in Wolfe, Capote, Mailer, and Didion are not just technically interesting devices of style, but enactments of value.

Works Cited

Index

Works Cited

Primary

Truman Capote

Other Voices, Other Rooms. New York: Random House, 1948.
A Tree of Night and Other Stories. New York: Random House, 1949.
The Grass Harp. New York: Random House, 1951.
The Muses Are Heard. New York: Random House, 1956.
In Cold Blood. New York: Random House, 1965.
The Dogs Bark. New York: Random House, 1973.
Music for Chameleons. New York: Random House, 1980.

Joan Didion

Slouching towards Bethlehem. New York: Farrar, Straus, and Giroux, 1968.
Play It As It Lays. New York: Farrar, Straus, and Giroux, 1970.
"Why I Write." *New York Times Book Review* 5 Dec. 1976: 2, 98–99. Reprinted in *Joan Didion: Essays and Conversations*. Ed. Ellen G. Friedman. Princeton: Ontario Review Press, 1984. 5–10. (References here are to Friedman.)
A Book of Common Prayer. New York: Simon and Schuster, 1977.
The White Album. New York: Simon and Schuster, 1979.
Salvador. New York: Simon and Schuster, 1979.
Democracy: A Novel. New York: Simon and Schuster, 1984.

Norman Mailer

Cannibals and Christians. New York: Dial Press, 1966.
The Armies of the Night. New York: New American Library, 1968.
Of a Fire on the Moon. Boston: Little Brown, 1969.
The Executioner's Song. Boston: Little Brown, 1979.

Tom Wolfe

The Kandy-Kolored Tangerine-Flake Streamline Baby. New York: Farrar, Straus, and Giroux, 1965.
The Electric Kool-Aid Acid Test. New York: Farrar, Straus, and Giroux, 1968.
"The New Journalism." In *The New Journalism*. Ed. Wolfe and E. W. Johnson. New York: Harper and Row, 1973. 3–52.
The Right Stuff. New York: Farrar, Straus, and Giroux, 1979.

Secondary

Aristotle. *The Rhetoric*. Trans. Lane Cooper. New York: Appleton, 1932.
Augustine. *On Christian Doctrine*. Trans. D. W. Roberts, Jr. Indianapolis: Library of the Liberal Arts, 1958.
Beard, Ruth. *An Outline of Piaget's Developmental Psychology for Students and Teachers*. New York: Basic Books, 1969.
Booth, Wayne C. *Modern Dogma and the Rhetoric of Assent*. Chicago: U of Chicago P, 1974.
———. *The Rhetoric of Fiction*. Chicago: U of Chicago P, 1961.
Brock, Bernard L., and Robert L. Scott, eds. *Methods of Rhetorical Criticism: A Twentieth Century Perspective*. 2nd. ed. Detroit: Wayne State UP, 1980.
Bryan, William Frank, and Ronald S. Crane, eds. *The English Familiar Essay*. New York: Athenum Press, 1916.
Burke, Kenneth. *A Grammar of Motives*. Berkeley: U of California P, 1969.
———. *A Rhetoric of Motives*. Berkeley: U of California P, 1969.
———. *The Rhetoric of Religion*. Boston: Beacon, 1961.
Carlyle, Thomas. "Characteristics." *The Works of Thomas Carlyle*. Ed. H. D. Traill. Centenary Edition. 30 vols. London: Chapman and Hall, 1896–1899. 28:2–43.
Cicero. *De Oratore*. Trans. E. W. Sutton. The Loeb Classical Library. Cambridge, Mass.: Harvard UP, 1942, 1948.

————. *Orator*. Trans. H. M. Hubbell. The Loeb Classical Library. Cambridge, Mass.: Harvard UP, 1942.

Corbett, Edward P. J. "The Rhetoric of the Closed Hand and the Rhetoric of the Open Fist." *College Composition and Communication* 20 (1969): 288–96.

Cowley, Malcom, ed. *Writers at Work*: The Paris Review *Interviews*. New York: Viking, 1960.

De Man, Paul. "The Rhetoric of Temporality." *Blindness and Insight*. Minneapolis: U of Minnesota P, 1983. 187–228.

Fielder, Leslie, ed. *The Art of the Essay*. 2nd ed. New York: Crowell, 1969.

Gibson, Walker, ed. *The Limits of Language*. New York: Hill and Wang, 1962.

Hellman, John. *Fables of Fact: The New Journalism as New Fiction*. Urbana: U of Illinois P, 1981.

Hollowell, John. *Fact and Fiction: The New Journalism and the Nonfiction Novel*. Chapel Hill: U of North Carolina P, 1977.

Iser, Wolfgang. *The Act of Reading: A Theory of Aesthetic Response*. Baltimore: Johns Hopkins UP, 1978.

James, William. *Psychology: A Briefer Course*. New York: Holt, 1892.

Johnson, Diane. "Death for Sale." Rev. of *The Executioner's Song*. *The New York Review of Books* 6 Dec. 1979: 3–5.

Kant, Immanuel. *Critique of Judgment*. Trans. J. H. Bernard. New York: Hafner, 1951.

Kazin, Alfred. *Bright Book of Life*. Boston: Little Brown, 1973.

Krim, Seymour. "The Newspaper as Literature/Literature as Leadership." *The Reporter as Artist: A Look at the New Journalism Controversy*. Ed. Ronald Weber. New York: Hastings House, 1974. 169–87.

Langbaum, Robert. *The Poetry of Experience*. New York: Norton, 1963.

Longinus. *On the Sublime*. Trans. W. Rhys Roberts. 2nd ed. Cambridge: Cambridge UP, 1907.

Martin, Stoddard. *California Writers*. London: Macmillan, 1983.

Orwell, George. "Politics and the English Language." *The Collected Essays, Journalism, and Letters of George Orwell*. Ed. Sonia Orwell and Ian Angus. 4 vols. New York: Harcourt, Brace, 1968. 4: 127–40.

Perelman, Chaim and L. Olbrechts-Tyteca. *The New Rhetoric: A Treatise on Argumentation*. Trans. John Wilkinson and Purcell Weaver. Notre Dame: Notre Dame UP, 1969.

Plato. *Phaedrus*. Trans. W. C. Helmbold and W. G. Rabinowitz. Indianapolis: Library of the Liberal Arts, 1956.

Plimpton, George. "The Story behind a Nonfiction Novel." *New York Times Book Review* 16 Jan. 1966: 2–3, 38–42.

Poirier, Richard. *Norman Mailer.* New York: Viking, 1972.

Polman, Dick. "'Squirrely little' Capote remembered in Kansas." Knight-Ridder Newspapers. Week of 10 Sept. 1984.

Rygiel, Dennis. "On the Neglect of Twentieth Century Nonfiction: A Writing Teacher's View." *College English* 46 (1984): 392–400.

Shahn, Ben. *The Shape of Content.* Cambridge, Mass.: Harvard UP, 1957.

Steiner, George. *Language and Silence: Essays on Language, Literature, and the Inhuman.* New York: Atheneum, 1967.

Tanner, Tony. *City of Words: American Fiction 1950–1970.* New York: Harper and Row, 1971.

———. "Death in Kansas." *Truman Capote's* In Cold Blood: *A Critical Handbook.* Ed. Irving Malin. Belmont, Calif.: Wadsworth, 1968.

Tennyson, G. B. *Sartor Called Resartus.* Princeton: Princeton UP, 1965.

Thomas, Lewis. *The Lives of a Cell.* New York: Viking, 1974.

———. *The Medusa and the Snail.* New York: Viking, 1979.

Wallace, Karl R. *Francis Bacon on Communication and Rhetoric.* Chapel Hill: U of North Carolina P, 1943.

Weaver, Richard. "The Spaciousness of the Old Rhetoric." *The Ethics of Rhetoric.* Chicago: Henry Regnery, 1953. 164–85.

———. *Language Is Sermonic.* Ed. Richard L. Johannesen et. al. Baton Rouge: Louisiana State UP, 1970.

Weber, Ronald. *The Literature of Fact: Literary Nonfiction in American Writing.* Athens: Ohio UP, 1980.

Williams, Joseph M. *Style: Ten Lessons in Clarity and Grace.* Glenview, Illinois: Scott Foresman, 1981.

Winchell, Mark Royden. *Joan Didion.* Twayne United States Authors Series. Boston: Twayne Publishers, 1980.

Young, Richard E., Alton L. Becker, and Kenneth L. Pike. *Rhetoric: Discovery and Change.* New York: Harcourt Brace, 1970.

Zavarzadeh, Mas'ud. *The Mythopoeic Reality: The Postwar American Nonfiction Novel.* Urbana: U of Illinois P, 1976.

Index

Metadiscourse, 5, 179; in Didion, 141, 149, 161; in Mailer, 89–93; in Wolfe, 9, 35, 46
Metonymy, 29, 34, 138
Montaigne, 142–44
Mystery. *See* Inexplicability; Silence, as rhetorical strategy; Sublime

New Journalism, 1, 2–3, 176–77; and Capote, 65–67; and Didion, 142, 144; and Wolfe, 8, 9, 22, 25, 44, 46
Nonfiction novel, 1, 48, 56, 65–67

Orwell, George, 143, 165–66, 169

Perelman, Chaim, 17–18, 22, 32, 36, 69, 78, 107, 113–15, 176
Piaget, Jean, 153
Pike, Kenneth L., 114–15
Plato, 59
Poirier, Richard, 95
Presence, rhetorical strategies for achieving, 17–18, 18–30, 32, 78, 152
"Pushing the outside of the envelope," 8–9, 16–17, 27, 42, 70, 97–98, 180

Repetition, as rhetorical strategy, 18–19, 27, 32, 109, 124
Reportage, 2–3, 177; and Capote, 56; and Didion, 142–44; and Mailer, 92–93, 115; and Wolfe, 15–16, 43
Rhetoric, 2–3, 177–78; Capote's use of, 81; Didion's use of, 161–73; Mailer's use of, 98–115; Wolfe's use of, 13, 29

Rhetorical criticism, 3, 99–100, 161–73
Rhetoric and composition, 6–7, 114–15
Rhetoric of particularity, 134–36
Rhetoric of process, 139–41

Scene-by-scene reconstruction, 39, 42, 43, 57, 177
Scott, Robert, 3
Silence, as rhetorical strategy: in Capote, 48–57, 70–81; in Didion, 136–39, 143, 144, 151; in Mailer, 116–18, 118–21, 129–32; in Wolfe, 12, 24, 35, 39
Silence, as theme, 57–67, 101
Status detail, 28, 33, 123, 134
Style, 1, 3, 4–5; Capote's, 56–57, 71–72, 76–77, 80–81; Didion's, 151, 159, 172; Mailer's, 88, 102, 117–18; Wolfe's, 37, 39, 44, 46
Style as argument, 6, 175–80; in Capote, 76, 80–81; in Didion, 172; in Mailer, 117–18; in Wolfe, 42, 46–47
Sublime, the, 5; in Capote, 69; in Didion, 152–53, 154; in Mailer, 83, 86, 87, 96; in Wolfe, 9–10, 17
Synecdoche, 29, 34, 138

Tanner, Tony, 37, 71
Thomas, Lewis, 4, 174–76

Weaver, Richard, 3, 43, 51, 100, 113–14, 115, 144, 177
Weber, Ronald, 2, 3, 74
White, E. B., 4, 143
Williams, Joseph M., 89

Wolfe, Tom, 1–7, 8–47, 69–70, 85, 88, 88–89, 96, 117–18, 144, 147, 149, 153, 154, 172, 174–80. Works: *The Electric Kool-Aid Acid Test,* 11–13, 23–26, 30, 40, 42, 43, 45, 73, 101; *The Kandy-Kolored Tangerine-Flake Streamline Baby,* 9, 17; "The Kandy-Kolored Tangerine-Flake Streamline Baby," 10–11, 31–32; "Las Vegas," 9, 18–22, 32; "The New Journalism," 2–3, 8, 17, 22, 25, 29, 33, 34, 39, 44, 142; *The Right Stuff,* 13–15, 26–29, 33, 34, 40, 44–45, 82, 97

Young, Richard E., 114–15

Zavarzadeh, Mas'ud, 2, 70–71, 122

CHRIS ANDERSON received his B.A. from Gonzaga University (1977) and his M.A. and Ph.D. from the University of Washington (1979, 1983). From 1982 to 1986 he was Assistant Professor of English and Co-director of Freshman English at the University of North Carolina, Greensboro. He is currently Assistant Professor of English and Composition Coordinator at Oregon State University. He has published articles in a number of journals, including *Christianity and Literature, Quarterly Journal of Speech, Prose Studies, Wordsworth Circle,* and *Studies in the Novel.* In 1984 he won the South Atlantic Modern Language Association's award for the best article of the year in the *South Atlantic Review.*